Contents

SO-AVW-983

Why Are Catholics So Concerned About Sin?

More Answers to Puzzling Questions
About the Catholic Church

AL KRESTA

SERVANT
BOOKS

PUBLISHED BY ST. ANTHONY MESSENGER PRESS
CINCINNATI, OHIO

RESCRIPT

In accord with the *Code of Canon Law,* I hereby grant my permission to publish the manuscript *Why Are Catholics So Concerned About Sin? And Answers to Other Questions About the Catholic Church* by Al Kresta.

> Most Reverend Daniel E. Pilarczyk
> Archbishop of the Archdiocese of Cincinnati
> Cincinnati, Ohio
> May 9, 2005

The permission to publish is a declaration that a book or pamphlet is considered to be free from doctrinal or moral error. It is not implied that those who have granted the permission to publish agree with the contents, opinions or statements expressed.

Unless otherwise noted, Scripture passages have been taken from the *Revised Standard Version,* Catholic edition. Copyright 1946, 1952, 1971 by the Division of Christian Education of the National Council of Churches of Christ in the USA. Used by permission. All rights reserved.

Catechism (CCC) quotations are taken from the *Catechism of the Catholic Church,* second edition revised in accordance with the official Latin text promulgated by Pope John Paul II (Libreria Editrice Vaticana, 1997).

Quotations of Vatican II documents are taken from Austin Flannery, ed., *Vatican Council II: The Conciliar and Post Conciliar Documents,* study edition (New York: Costello, 1986).

Cover design by Brian Fowler
Book design by Phillips Robinette, O.F.M.

Library of Congress Cataloging-in-Publication Data

Kresta, Al.
  Why are Catholics so concerned about sin? : more answers to puzzling questions about the Catholic Church / Al Kresta.
     p. cm.
  Includes index.
  ISBN 0-86716-696-7 (pbk. : alk. paper) 1. Catholic Church—Doctrines—Miscellanea.
I. Title.

BX1754.3.K73 2005
282—dc22

                              2005014534

ISBN 0-86716-696-7

Copyright ©2005 by Al Kresta. All rights reserved.

Published by Servant Books, an imprint of St. Anthony Messenger Press
28 W. Liberty St.
Cincinnati, OH 45202
www.AmericanCatholic.org

Printed in the United States of America

Printed on acid-free paper

05 06 07 08 09 5 4 3 2 1

$\mathcal{A}$cknowledgments and Dedications

The original deadline for this book—a promised follow-up to my first volume, *Why Do Catholics Genuflect?*—was Monday, February 17, 2003. It wasn't finished, and I was ready to beg my editor for more time. But God, the devil or nature (the three are not equally privileged causes) gave me one of the best excuses a man could have.

That night my wife rushed me to the emergency room. *Necrotizing fasciitis,* the regularly fatal "flesh-eating bacteria," had placed me on their menu. These invisible beasts had penetrated my skin and were gorging themselves like locusts on young cereal crops, all the while making haste to poison my blood.

The next day a group of doctors at St. Joseph Mercy Hospital in Ann Arbor, Michigan, clustered around my bed and told me that the only deadline I might reach that day had to do with the Book of Life. I hadn't expected, nor was I especially eager to, meet my ultimate Editor. But to save my life the surgeons would have to amputate my left leg above the knee, now raising the embarrassing question, *how* does this Catholic genuflect?

The Divine Editor showed me such mercy that my earthly editors felt the only gracious move was to extend their deadline. Another two years would pass before I managed to get the manuscript ready for publication.

I may yet, Lord willing, tell that story of February 2003 in writing. But in case I don't, I want to dedicate this book to all (you know who you are) who kept vigil, offered Masses on my behalf, unfurled a life-size image of Our Lady of Guadalupe in the hospital waiting room, signed prayer petitions at local conferences, built ramps for my wheelchair, trained me to walk well enough to escort my daughter down the aisle at her wedding, kept my family in meals and tender embraces, answered questions for curious journalists, filled in for me on the air, donated money and vegetables, baby-sat our younger children, wrote letters, sent cards, visited and even stopped to introduce your children to "the guy on the radio who was raised from the dead." Your countless hugs, handshakes and hallelujahs formed a web of affirmation and love that will never leave me. I am utterly convinced that without your prayers, I would not be on the earth to dedicate this book.

Sally and I cannot possibly repay you in this world. We can, however, continue to try and do our part in bearing witness to our common faith in the risen Lord, which we share with all the patriarchs, prophets, apostles, martyrs, teachers and the faithful footstep followers of Jesus Christ from every generation, nation, kindred and tongue.

About this Book

While the range of questions in this book is not quite as broad as *Why Do Catholics Genuflect?*, I generally deal with them more thoroughly. A number of them treat the meeting of God at the end of history and at the end of a life of rejecting his grace. While the presentation of the book is primarily doctrinal exposition and apologetics rather than autobiography, I won't deny that my week of unconsciously hovering between life and death sharpened my confidence in the goodness of God and his divine mercy, as well as my awareness of the shocking possibility of eternal separation from him.

This book is certainly a potpourri rather than a work of systematic theology. Certain of these questions only arise in conversation with particular segments of the Christian world: for example, "Are Catholics saved?" Elsewhere I try to illuminate more commonly asked questions, such as "Isn't hell a bit of overkill?" In all I have tried to faithfully present historic Catholic teaching.

As in *Why Do Catholics Genuflect?* I cite many passages of Scripture. Over the years I've heard Christians of a certain bent deplore this constant reference to Scripture as illegitimate "proof-texting." It is a strange charge. Would one prefer to be ignorant of the relevant passages?

Citing sources shows elementary respect for the reader. When discussing theories of knowledge, I'm glad to see Plato's presentation of his allegory of the cave cited as *Republic*, 508–515. Or if struggling through the dense philosophical debate over "hermeneutics," I would feel cheated if the author didn't clue me in to his reliance on Gadamer's *Truth and Method,* II.II.2c.

When it comes to Scripture, however, the rules seem to change. Cheeks become flushed and nostrils flare when specific passages are cited. Perhaps it is because those so inflamed imagine that the citation of a biblical source is a cheap attempt to clinch an argument with a resounding appeal to divine revelation. "How unfair! Who can argue with God?"

But this assumes that the author believes that there is such a thing as an uninterpreted text. While this may be true of certain Muslims and some fundamentalist Protestants, it is not the case with most writers on things spiritual. Even divinely revealed texts require interpretation. The argument is over whether or not one's interpretation is justified.

One may disagree with the relevance or weight given to a particular passage of Scripture, but to regard the invocation of Scripture as illegitimate is contrary to the standard practice of writers, who feel obliged to disclose their debts as well as their sources. And remember, the Scripture is the primary "document," the public revelation, of the Christian faith recognized by Catholics, Protestants and Eastern Orthodox as well as those believers who try to escape labels by adopting the label "non-denominational." (*Non-denominational* simply defines a community that hasn't existed long enough to acknowledge its interpretive tradition or spawn new churches that need a name. Having pastored a "non-denominational" church, I might be forgiven this poke at myself. While the Catholic church in America is experiencing a shortage of vocations to the priesthood, there is no shortage of those feeling called to the papacy, myself included.)

A Christian book dealing with questions of sin and its consequences must rely on the narrative of man's origin and fall in the Book of Genesis. Whenever the story of Creation and the Fall is invoked, however, someone will ask how Genesis squares with science. Good question, but this book isn't the place for it. While I respect the efforts of paleontologists, physical anthropologists and evolutionary psychologists, the biological origins of man have little bearing on my discussion of our first parents, Adam and Eve, and their introduction of sin into human experience.

Genesis itself recognizes that God "formed man from the dust of the ground." That is, the formation of the human body derives, in some way, from the natural history of the earth. It is enough for my purposes in this book to echo the *Catechism of the Catholic Church* when it refers to the Fall as a "primeval event…narrated in figurative language in the Book of Genesis" (*CCC,* glossary; see #390).

That human beings are "fallen" is, perhaps, the most easily observed and self-evident of the Christian doctrines. This experience of human sinfulness is in no way challenged by various anthropological theories of hominid development. G.K. Chesterton wrote of the human race's sense of sin was:

> …a product of spiritual conviction; it had nothing to do with remote physical origins. Men thought mankind wicked because they felt wicked themselves. If a man feels wicked, I cannot see why he should suddenly feel good because somebody tells him that his ancestors once had tails. Man's primary purity and innocence may have dropped off with his tail, for all anybody knows; the only thing we all know about that primary purity and innocence is that we have not got it.… By its nature the evidence of Eden is something that one cannot find. By its nature the evidence of sin is something that one cannot help finding.[1]

Introduction

Why do Catholics make so much of sin?

Do we? It seems to me that through most of my lifetime the word *sin,* even for many American Catholics, has been losing its usefulness.

The seven deadly sins[1] were once considered the bane of civilization, as destructive for individuals and society as smoking and racial segregation are considered today. These sins were woven through the popular piety of Catholic Europe, inspiring poets and artists. Chaucer included a long sermon on the seven deadly sins in "The Parson's Tale" in his *Canterbury Tales.* In Dante's *Divine Comedy* the terraces of purgatory are patterned on the seven deadly sins. Giotto, Lorenzetti, Bosch and Breughel the Elder all portrayed the seven deadly sins in their art. The concept of sin was meaningful and held cultural currency.

Today our public storytelling and cultural judgments still regard some of the deadly sins as shameful. "Greed is good," proclaims Gordon Gecko in the movie *Wall Street,* but his reptilian name and eventual arrest warn us that greed is not good. The nineteenth- and early twentieth-century imperialism of the Western nations is now commonly regarded as the deadly sins of pride and greed writ large on the canvas of world history.

Yet some of the deadly sins meet with cultural approval and are even championed as liberation and encouraged by global corporations. Anger, for instance, is often acted out in violence. There is no serious debate among psychologists and sociologists that childhood viewing of television violence increases the likelihood of later criminal behavior, yet aspiring screenwriters, eager producers, hungry actors, powerful studios and extensive distribution networks continue to provide programs that amuse approving viewers with gratuitous violence. Aggressive advertising encourages gluttony, envy, sloth and lust, even as we lament obesity, theft, disloyalty to employers and single-parent households.

Even when acts are recognized as wrong, distasteful or politically incorrect, they are not commonly described as transgressions of God's will. Sloth might signal a need for antidepressants; pride might be a recipe for success; gluttony is an eating disorder; anger is managed, not confessed; lust adorns our billboards and is celebrated as liberation from repressive taboos. Most discussion of the other deadly personal and social dysfunctions occurs without reference to sin or divine law.

Another way of discounting sin is by regarding it as a quaint notion, as in Hawthorne's *The Scarlet Letter.* Our culture distances it from us, as when we refer to Bible-thumping fundamentalists or knuckle-rapping nuns. They give sin a bad name! Who wants to sound like them?

Sometimes we neuter sin's sting by reducing it to a list of misbehaviors that our political opponents support or protect. For the political right, liberals destroy through abortion and homosexuality. For the political left, conservatives destroy by being jingoistic, protective of corporate power and unconsciously ethnocentric. Nevertheless, as Solzhenitsyn warned, sin is not to be identified as the province of others. The line that divides sinners from saints runs right down the middle of each human heart.

Of course, removing *sin* from our collective vocabularies or assigning it to passé religious traditions doesn't alter the dehumanizing realities the word is meant to describe.

The ethical scandals in corporate America, the epidemic of STDs, the indifference to daily starvation of children, the shedding of innocent blood in abortion, divorce and serial adultery, a growing disparity between rich and poor, falsifying research, frivolous lawsuits, the breakdown of the natural family, lying, double-crossing, cheating, hoarding, abuse of mind-altering substances—all create social disasters as well as private tragedies. Such sins strangle God's life in us and stifle his plan for our lives. They deprive us of all we were created to be and frustrate the achievement of the best version of ourselves. Because of sin we fail to become what we were born to be, and then we aren't the gift we ought to be in serving others.

Sin ruptures our relationship with God, turns us against ourselves, alienates us from others and even introduces disharmony into our natural environment (see Genesis 3:1–19; Romans 8:18–25). Sin leads to death and thwarts God's purpose of drawing us into his Trinitarian life of love (Romans 6:23; Ephesians 2:1–2; see also *Catechism of the Catholic Church,* #1849–1876). Most simply, sin means deliberately falling short of the will of God—who created us, who plans our supreme good and wants to share his life with us.

God, Creation and Truth

In his book *Know Why You Believe,* Paul E. Little quotes Mortimer Adler's explanation for the essay on God from the monumental *Great Books of the Western World.* Adler, the editor, says that with the exception of a few mathematicians and physicists, all the authors of the "great books" are represented in this chapter about God. "In sheer quantity of references, as well as in variety, this is the largest chapter [of the introductory synopticon]. The reason is obvious. More consequences for thought and action follow the affirmation or denial of God than from answering any other basic question.

Little says that "Adler goes on to spell out the practical implications: the whole tenor of human life is affected by whether people regard themselves as supreme beings in the universe or acknowledge a superhuman being whom they conceive of as an object of fear or love, a force to be defined or a Lord to be obeyed."[2]

Discourse on God is the largest single discussion in the intellectual tradition of the West.

When we survey the intellectual landscape and see through the centuries the discarded and failed hypotheses and the opposing paths of ingenious but futile philosophical trails and broken chains of reason, we could easily lose heart. Many contemporary philosophers have, like disappointed lovers, turned their backs on the quest for truth and ultimate reality. They've abandoned hope of ever attaining a glimpse of God's view of things. For these postmodernists, poststructuralists, deconstructionists and neo-pragmatists, there are only many truths and even many realities. Truth becomes merely the compliment we pay to sentences that work for us.[3]

This is ultimately a counsel of despair that will not lead to human flourishing. It mockingly portrays our noblest aspirations for love, truth, significance and justice as forms of self-deception. People will make great sacrifices for what they believe is true; they won't for what they are told is ultimately false or illusory.

But we can take heart. Looking over the graveyard of competing philosophies, we note that they divide into two opposing but basic possibilities: God exists or God does not exist. A further clarifying occurs when we ask, "If God exists, is he personal? Or, is 'it' impersonal?"

When Catholics say, "I believe in God, the Father Almighty, maker of heaven and earth," they make a radical but rational statement. They assert the primacy of meaning over matter. Life is not merely matter in motion, a secondary byproduct of natural forces. Life emerges from the creation as the result of God's free thought. Further, God is a society of Persons, the Triune God whose character is love and goodness. Moreover, being made in his image, we can think his thoughts after him, making "science"—knowledge about ourselves, history and his cosmos—possible. The cosmos is so ordered that we can intellectually comprehend it. God is good as well as rational, love as well as *logos*. The ultimate reality is the infinite-personal who reveals himself in creation and redemption.

God's Image Revealed

Before I go any further, let me say what may seem obvious: atheists can certainly live moral lives. Even those who deny God's existence, after all, are created in the image and likeness of God, and they must judge right from wrong, good from evil, truth from falsity. Humans are not only meaning-seeking creatures but morally judging ones.

Materialists would deny, however, that their advocacy of civil rights or creation of hospitals points toward their creation in the image of God. They see morality as just an aid to survival and reproduction. The adoption of these moral causes, they would argue, has evolutionary survival value. Equality and compassionate care are social goods that advantage us over less social and less neurologically complex animals. Rape, child abuse and torture are taboo because the race in its collective wisdom and experience realize that these are socially destructive behaviors.

This is fine as far as it goes. But perhaps an individual finds survival value in racial discrimination, double-crossing, cheating, rape, torture or child abuse. If one has a taste or a need for such behaviors and can escape the social consequences of breaking these taboos, then why isn't he or she justified in pursuing the behavior?

If God does not exist, there is no transcendent right and wrong by which we should form our consciences; there is only social conditioning. Even atheists, however, live as though some things are truly wrong, while love, sacrifice, pursuit of truth and human equality are truly right. This is inconsistent with a materialistic view of things, which denies God's existence and the objectivity of moral claims.

Atheist and Princeton philosopher Peter Singer, having denied that human beings have any rights derived from God, insists that we grant rights to animals. Failing to do so, Singer accuses, amounts to speciesism.[4] From a Catholic perspective, when Adam was given dominion over God's creation, his task was to image God to the entire creation. He mediated between God and material creatures, since he himself was an immaterial and material unity. To the earth, the fish, birds and land animals, he was the cultivator, not the destroyer, called to bring all creation to the fullness of its nature. The whole logic of Christianity is one of the higher serving the lower and the strong protecting the weak.

This is even more so with fellow human beings. Human dignity and the sanctity of life find their justification in the Catholic doctrine of divine creation. When Adam first laid eyes on Eve, the Hebrew of Genesis 2:23 makes it clear that he spoke poetry. He recognized a match for himself, someone who was to be valued for her own sake, someone with intrinsic worth because she had been given existence to image God.

Sometimes this is best realized in the breach. For instance, to murder a man is to execute God in effigy. To violate a person is to violate God (see Genesis 9:6). Since the person is made for his own sake and not for any utilitarian end, he must not be used as property.

In the Incarnation God tangibly and unqualifiedly aligns himself with every single person, thereby declaring that every human person is of infinite worth. "Even the hairs of your head are all numbered. Fear not; you are of more value than many sparrows" (Luke 12:7). If man was to cultivate the earth, how much more his responsibility to his fellow man? The sanctity of human life must be protected against every ideology, from the political right or left, and every force that would cheapen or diminish human life.

This denial of the objective truth and morality by which we enhance and protect human dignity has a familiar, beguiling sound. In *Back to Methuselah* George Bernard Shaw has the serpent tempting Eve: "You see things; and you say 'Why?' But I dream things that never were; and I say 'Why not?'"[5] This is not the promise of creativity; it is the lure of fantasy to replace reality.

The core of sin is not imagination or sex or veneration of some aspect of the created order, for it is right and natural to honor the good, the true and the beautiful. The essence of sin is the turning from reality to illusion, the refusal to acknowledge God's moral order. In short, it is the denial of God's Word, the Word by which he created the universe and ordered the cosmos, the Word by which he moved the prophets to speak and write, the Word which took on human flesh and which consecrates the divine food, the Eucharist. This word is spoken for our flourishing.

An Unfair Inheritance?

Shortly after the beginning of the human race, Adam and Eve ignored God and invented their own truth, their own norms for good and evil, their own vision of reality. Postmodernists might find this an interesting project, but isn't it simply narcissism made respectable, solipsism made tolerable, a pluralism without any hope of understanding others since we are locked up in our own heads?

When faced with the serpentine temptation, Adam and Eve simply lived as though God didn't exist and had never spoken. And they have infected all those descended from them with the same tendency (Romans 5:12–20; 1 Corinthians 15:21–22).

I've often heard the complaint "How unfair! Why should I inherit the effects of Adam's sin?" In a culture in which we so prize individualism, the doctrine of original sin confronts us with the reminder that we are not self-created, autonomous, individual units. We are a solidarity, a corporate personality, not a collection of solitaries. Though some seem to think that they were born without navels, others conceive, birth, teach, protect, humor, employ, heal, marry, baptize and bury us. All through our lives we rest in a web of interdependent relationships. Others pass on to us and we pass on to them both good and ill.

Who knows this better than parents and teachers when they pause to consider their importance? In psychology we have the phenomenon of the "looking-glass self," which observes that, for better or worse, we conceive of ourselves and define ourselves largely through our most important relationship with another—be it spouse, parent, employer or God. Others form our identities.

I never say much about the unearned benefits I receive from society. When I turn on the lights in my office, I don't think of offering thanksgiving to Edison for the lightbulb. But, sinner that I am, I grouse, murmur and complain when I experience the negative consequences of others' behavior. When it comes to recognizing the consequences of Adam's sin in my life, I think: What did I do to deserve this?

First of all, nothing. Just as I didn't merit the poor eyesight or the capacity for quick verbal associations that my father's side passed on to me. Just as I did nothing to merit the blessings of electricity.

Second, actually, quite a bit. I commit actual sin and thereby ratify and perpetuate Adam's pattern, proving that I am of his kind. I don't necessarily follow Edison's pattern of brilliant invention. Don't I "deserve" my position in Adam at least as much as I deserve my position in Edison? The human race is a solidarity, one community, and our individual actions shape and mold those around us. Some individuals by virtue of their moment in history, their genius or their depravity are more influential than others. Adam influenced everyone.

The good news is that Christ's work of healing is potentially as universal and far more contagious than Adam's infection. As far as the disease is spread, so far spreads the cure. Or as Corrie ten Boom wrote: "There is no pit in which the love of God is not deeper still."[6]

Woe to Me

Anyone who tries to talk about "sin and salvation" today is handicapped by a vocabulary that many intended readers regard as religious jargon. *Expiation, justification, second advent, rite of reconciliation, sacrament of the Eucharist* and *mortal and venial sin* have all come to sound like ethnic jive, not the language of the dominant culture. These terms sound alien, even alienating, to the uninitiated. Yet to be silent about sin is neither wise nor loving.

Søren Kierkegaard noted this in his parable of the circus clown and the fire. Joseph Cardinal Ratzinger, now Pope Benedict XVI, drew from this story in his *Introduction to Christianity,* first published in 1968:

> According to this story a traveling circus in Denmark had caught fire. The manager thereupon sent the clown, who was already dressed and made-up for the performance, into the neighbouring village to fetch help, especially as there was a danger that the fire would spread across the fields of dry stubble and engulf the village itself. The clown hurried into the village and requested the inhabitants to come as quickly as possible to the blazing circus and help to put the fire out. But the villagers took the clown's shouts simply for an excellent piece of advertising, meant to attract as many people as possible to the performance; they applauded the clown and laughed till they cried. The clown felt more like weeping than laughing; he tried in vain to get people to be serious, to make it clear to them that it was no trick but bitter earnest, that there really was a fire. His supplications only increased the laughter; people thought he was playing his part splendidly—until finally the fire did engulf the village, it was too late for help and both circus and village were burned to the ground.[7]

When a family's house is billowing smoke from the attic vents, it's not love but timidity and indifference that prevent us from rushing to their front door screaming, "Fire! Fire!" Sin simmers, smolders and sometimes blazes through human lives, leaving a charred trail of destruction. Those who can show the scars that come from playing with fire owe the rest of us a warning even if we sound like fools.

Speak we must in the face of disbelief and a million distractions. "Woe to me if I do not preach the gospel!" (1 Corinthians 9:16). "For I am not ashamed of the gospel: it is the power of God for salvation to every one who has faith…. For in it the righteousness [justice] of God is revealed…as it is written, 'He who through faith is righteous [just] shall live'" (Romans 1:16, 17).

That which was from the beginning, which we have heard, which we have seen with our eyes, which we have looked upon and touched with our hands, concerning the word of life—the life was made manifest, and we saw it, and testify to it, and proclaim to you the eternal life which was with the Father and was made manifest to us—that which we have seen and heard we proclaim also to you, so that you may have fellowship with us; and our fellowship is with the Father and with his Son Jesus Christ. And we are writing this that our joy may be complete. (1 John 1:1–4)

Part I

Teaching Authority

Do Catholics believe that the Bible is the inspired Word of God?

> The divinely revealed realities, which are contained and presented in the text of sacred Scripture, have been written down under the inspiration of the Holy Spirit.... In the sacred books the Father who is in heaven comes lovingly to meet his children, and talks with them; and the force in the Word of God is so great that it remains the support and energy of the Church, the strength of faith for her children, the food of the soul, the pure and perennial source of spiritual life. (*Dei verbum,* 11, 21)[1]

God has spoken in countless situations and in a variety of forms. Some heard God speak directly: some dreamed dreams, and others saw visions and images. God has spoken through historical events like the Exodus and personal dramas like those of Hosea. He has spoken in poetry and oracle through prophets like Isaiah and Amos, and he has spoken through written texts like the letters of Saint Paul.

The Bible records these divine-human communications. Yet Scripture is far more than a digest of human reflections and religious experiences. It is a creation of God.

Today's religious marketplace commonly over-promises. The campaigners of novel spiritual movements (which are simply fledgling organized religions) claim divine encounters that belittle by neglect the encounters of thousands who have lived and written from within four thousand years of the Abrahamic tradition. Part of this longstanding Abrahamic tradition is "inscripturation"—that is, the confidence that God not only gives an experience of himself but also the words to describe it. Catholics, and most Christians, believe that the phenomenon of an authoritative text is willed by God. To be as direct as possible: God is the principal author of Scripture.

Some would claim that it is impossible for the infinite God to reveal himself through finite humans. But why would God deny himself the capacity to convey himself and information about his cosmos through language formed by creatures made in his image? He is quite capable of revealing himself accurately, though not exhaustively.

"All Scripture is God-breathed" (2 Timothy 3:16, *New International Version*), or as the *Catechism of the Catholic Church* puts it: "Sacred Scripture is the speech of God as it is put down in writing under the breath of the Holy Spirit" (*CCC*, #81, quoting *Dei verbum*, 9). When humans speak, their words ride upon their breath. So too with God. His Spirit (Greek *pneuma*—that is, "breath") carries his Word. Since God is the author of Scripture, Catholics are to venerate it as they venerate the Lord's Body (*CCC*, #103).

The Catholic church doesn't insist on a particular theory of divine inspiration.[2] She teaches the doctrine without specifying how it took place. She does, however, insist on human participation. "To compose the sacred books, God chose certain men who, all the while he employed them in this task, made full use of their own faculties and powers so that, though he acted in them and by them, it was as true authors that they consigned to writing whatever he wanted written, and no more" (*Dei verbum*, 11, as quoted in *CCC*, #106).

This is unlike automatic writing or New Age channeling, which bypass the humanity of the medium and presume to be a direct dictation (sometimes called the "boss and stenographer" theory of inspiration) from some disembodied spirit. Human agency is critical to inspiration. Paul of Tarsus can be said to be the true author of Second Corinthians. Luke the physician is truly the author of the Gospel of Luke and Acts.

On the other hand, inspired Scripture is much more than the product of individual human genius, like Dante's *Divine Comedy,* Michelangelo's *Pieta* or the collective brilliance of the Human Genome Project. This is why every reading of Scripture during Mass ends with "The Word of the Lord," not "The word of Nehemiah" or "The word of Luke" or "The word of Moses."

Christians agree that as the Holy Spirit moved the human writers, he employed their language, background and skills. For instance, Luke has an outstanding command of the Greek language. His vocabulary is extensive and rich, and his style at times approaches that of classical Greek.

Again the Holy Spirit's superintendence did not rule out the human author's background or his human effort. Luke tells us, for instance, that in composing his Gospel and the Acts of the Apostles, he carefully investigated the story of Jesus and the early church. He states his literary intention: "to compile a narrative" rooted in the testimony of "those who from the beginning were eyewitnesses and ministers of the word." It seems good to him—since he, personally, has "followed all things closely for some time past"—to draw on his own insight and experience. He also states the purpose of his "orderly account": to insure that his readers "know the truth concerning the things of which you have been informed" (Luke 1:1–4). Luke believed that accuracy and reliability were necessary to justify the Christian truth claim. The Holy Spirit used his diligence.

Luke's writing may also reflect his training as a physician (see Colossians 4:14). While Mark tells us that the hemorrhaging woman suffered much at the hands of many physicians, Luke is a bit more restrained and protective of his fellow physicians, writing that she "could not be healed by any one" (see Mark 5:26; Luke 8:43). According to Luke, the physician, she was simply incurable.

Luke is also the only Gospel writer who mentions that Christ's agony in the garden produced sweat "like great drops of blood" (Luke 22:44). Is this the dangerous condition known as hematidrosis, the effusion of blood in one's perspiration caused by extreme anguish or strain? Capillaries dilate and burst, and blood mingles with sweat. Christ did confess that his distress had brought him to the threshold of death, but Luke is the only writer to describe an accompanying medical symptom (see Matthew 26:38; Mark 14:34; Hebrews 12:3–4).

When Peter's mother came down with a fever, only Luke mentions that it was a "high" fever and notes the means Jesus used to heal her (see Luke 4:39). Thus Luke's writings sound like those of Doctor Luke, the traveling companion of Paul, rather than some impersonal oracle.[3]

The Catholic understanding of inspiration is consistent with our understanding of human salvation. God is salvaging and redeeming the entire person—body, soul, mind and spirit—not abolishing the person or any of these faculties. Redemption perfects creation, and grace builds on nature.

Further, Catholics draw an analogy between the inscripturated Word (Scripture) and the incarnate Word (Jesus). "Indeed the words of God, expressed in the words of men, are in every way like human language, just as the Word of the eternal Father, when he took on himself the flesh of human weakness, became like men" (*CCC,* #101, quoting *Dei verbum,* 13). In spite of taking on human weakness, Jesus doesn't teach deceptively. Likewise, God doesn't lie when speaking in the human authors of Scripture.

We might have a difficult time hearing the Word of God in Scripture's genealogies, census statistics, ancient priestly codes for burning the fat off goats' kidneys, unfamiliar poetic forms and meters, brutal tales of conquest and distant cultural

customs. But with similar skepticism many first-century residents of Palestine couldn't grasp how a wandering Jewish field
preacher, standing so many inches high and weighing so many
pounds, eating fish and pita and walking and sleeping in their
midst, could have been the Word of God.

Nevertheless, Jesus spoke divine truth without error. So too
does Scripture. "All that the inspired authors or sacred writers
affirm should be regarded as affirmed by the Holy Spirit," and
the books of Scripture "firmly, faithfully, and without error teach
that truth which God, for the sake of our salvation, wished to
see confided to the Sacred Scriptures" (*Dei verbum,* 11).

The Catholic church maintains inspiration and inerrancy
without believing that the Bible is a scientific or historical text-
book. Galileo drew from the words of Cardinal Cesare
Baronius (1538–1607), a church historian highly esteemed in
Galileo's time: "The Bible tells us how to go to heaven, not
how the heavens go."[4]

We ought to receive the Old and New Testaments whole
and entire, in all their parts, as the literary expression of the
Word of God, just as we receive Jesus as the incarnate Word of
God (see John 20:31; 2 Timothy 3:16; 2 Peter 1:19–21; 3:15, 16).
"For ignorance of the Scripture," Saint Jerome taught, "is igno-
rance of Christ."[5]

*D*o Catholics take the Bible literally?

As literally as the many biblical authors intended their writings
to be taken! Because God reveals himself in humanly composed texts, Scripture demands attention as a work of literature
with all its literary forms and historical settings.

Bible is from the Latin *biblia,* which means "book." But

before it was ever called "The Book," it was a hefty collection of writings, a library. In this library we find all types of literature: historical narratives, legal texts, proverbs, poetry, prophecy, parables, allegory, sagas, letters, sermons, speeches and apocalypses. For this reason Catholics begin Scripture study by establishing the literal sense.

Literal is not literalistic. When Christ said, "I am the door," nobody reached for a knob at his navel. A literal reading of the text means reading it as the author intended and attending to the author's use of figurative language, analogies, symbolic numbers, types, proverbs, clichés, parables, legends and so forth.

For example, when we read in 1 and 2 Kings, "David was king of Israel," we comprehend it with the same degree of "literalness" as when reading Caesar's *Gallic Wars,* "All Gaul is divided into three parts." If, however, a story begins, "Once upon a time…" we know we are dealing with a fairy tale. A literal reading of *Cinderella* shouldn't give rise to archaeological digs searching for graves of the wicked sisters or the shards of the glass slipper. Reading the Psalms or *Cinderella* or 1 Kings or *How the Irish Saved Civilization* or Genesis or the editorial page of *The Washington Post* "literally" means, first off, discerning the document's literary genre and the author's intent.

When the literary form or style of a passage is not gauged, we not only misinterpret the Word of God but also do human damage. Let me give a few examples.

How many burdened parents have increased their suffering by misunderstanding Proverbs 22:6: "Train up a child in the way he should go, and when he is old he will not depart from it"? This is a proverb, not a promise. A proverb is a pithy saying that offers a general observation about life that is accepted by most people as true and helpful. Proverbs are not ironclad promises of what will or must take place if certain conditions are met. Yet how many parents have tortured themselves or blamed God when an adult child left the faith, because they thought this verse was an absolute promise whose conditions they failed to meet or that God failed to fulfill.

Proverbs frequently contradict one another, and their proper applications require wisdom. For instance, "Look before you leap" violates "He who hesitates is lost." Even in Scripture contradictory proverbs can be found sitting next to each other, glaring like snarling siblings: "Answer not a fool according to his folly, / lest you be like him yourself. Answer a fool according to his folly, / lest he be wise in his own eyes" (Proverbs 26:4–5).

One of the most famous and tragically misinterpreted verses is Matthew 27:25. Here Pilate declares that he finds nothing in Jesus worthy of death. The Jewish mob, whipped up by their leaders, then claim responsibility and pronounce a curse on themselves: "His blood be on us and our children." This verse has been wrongly invoked as a justification for violence against Jewish communities.

Notice that Matthew simply *describes* what the mob said; he doesn't *prescribe* that God or anybody else cooperate with their irresponsible oath. The followers of Jesus have no responsibility or permission to carry out the curses that foolish people call down on themselves.

God doesn't promise to respect or honor hasty vows. No action had to follow from this verse at all! A riotous group is manipulated into roaring a reckless oath. Nothing new here. Furthermore,

> …it is certainly only the Jews of that generation—and indeed, only *some* of them—who were responsible for the death of Jesus, not the Jews of later centuries. And that generation (and their children if they must be included despite Jer 31:30; Ezek 18:19–32) could from Matthew's perspective easily have been regarded as suffering God's judgment in the fall of Jerusalem when it occurred. This

verse was not intended to encourage Christians to bring vengeance upon the Jews. The Lord says "vengeance is mine" (Deut 32:35; Rom 12:19; Heb 10:30), and Christians taught by Jesus will love their "enemies" (5:11, 44; Rom 12:19–21).... Jesus has forgiven those responsible for his death (cf. Luke 23:34; the "ignorance" motif is picked up in Acts 3:14–17; 1 Cor 2:8), and God continues to love the Jews and will yet remember his covenant loyalty to them (cf. 23:39; but more clearly, Rom 11:26–32).[6]

We must respect the linguistic conventions of the historical period in which the piece was written. Scripture contains hyperbole or overstatement. Hyperbole is a figure of speech that exaggerates to make its point. We may not know how to pronounce the word, but we use hyperbole regularly in our conversations. "I'm so tired, I'm dead," or, "I'd give my whole fortune for a bowl of bean soup."

Jesus uses hyperbole when he says, "If your hand causes you to sin, cut it off.... If your foot causes you to sin, cut it off.... If your eye causes you to sin, pluck it out; it is better for you to enter the kingdom of God with one eye than with two eyes to be thrown into hell" (Mark 9:43–47; see Matthew 5:27–30; 18:6, 8–9). Jesus is not prescribing self-mutilation, since even a blind man can lust and a sticky-fingered thief who maims himself can still envy another's jewelry. The lesson? Sometimes sin can only be overcome by radical "spiritual surgery." Drastic action, not disfigurement, is the medicine for what ails the person addicted to sin.

The early Christian teacher Origen (c. 185–254) was brilliant, austere and so rigorous that he castrated himself in accordance with a literalistic reading of Matthew 19:12, "There are eunuchs who have made themselves eunuchs for the sake of the kingdom of heaven. He who is able to receive this, let him receive it."[7]

Origen's was a literalistic rather than a literal reading of the text. He ignored both the use of figurative speech and the context of the marriage and divorce discussion in which verse 12 is embedded. "Making oneself a eunuch" is a metaphor for choosing a life of celibacy. (By the way, in the fourth century the priesthood was opened to men born as eunuchs and those who suffered castration at the hands of others. Those who emasculated themselves, however, were permanently barred from ordination.)[8]

The literal sense of Scripture recognizes the extravagance of hyperbole as well as symbols, metaphors, proverbial expressions and so on. Each text must be interpreted according to its literary form, always respecting the author's intention, life situation and historical and cultural circumstances. The forest must not be missed for the trees, however. God is telling a unified, coherent story through Scripture that climaxes with the era of the new creation established by Christ. We must read Scripture with a view to the overarching storyline.

Historically, Catholics seek the *sensus plenior,* the "full sense" of Scripture. To arrive at the full meaning of Scripture, Catholics employ the "fourfold sense" of Scripture. Actually, there are two fundamental senses of Scripture: the literal and the spiritual, with three senses falling under the umbrella of the spiritual (the allegorical, the moral and the anagogical). But "all other senses of Sacred Scripture are based on the literal."[9]

The allegorical sense is sometimes called the typological. Through it we "acquire a more profound understanding of events by recognizing their significance in Christ" (*CCC,* #117; see #115–119). For instance, the crossing of the Red Sea and the entry into the Promised Land is a sign or type of deliverance from sin through baptism and into the kingdom of God. The fulfillment of a type is always more glorious, more powerful and more effective than the type itself.

There is also the "moral sense," which simply asks the question, "How does this passage lead me to act justly?" Lastly, there is the "anagogical sense," in which the events in the text are seen in their eternal significance. "How does this passage lead me toward the heavenly Jerusalem?" "A medieval couplet summarizes the four senses: 'The Letter speaks of deeds; Allegory to faith; The Moral how to act; Anagogy our destiny'" (*CCC,* #118).[10]

But back to the question, "Do Catholics interpret the Bible literally?" Yes, of necessity. The literal sense keeps our Bible study from deteriorating into a matter of saying, "This is what it means to me." Scripture is not clay that we can mold any way we like. It has firm, objective meaning. We aren't free to invent something that is not in the text or to ignore what is there. Because, after all, we all will be judged by what it says, not by what we wish it said. The literal sense keeps us honest in our interpretation.

Another way to find riches in Scripture and not just fool's gold is to consult with all the prospectors who have mined there before. The nineteenth-century English Baptist preacher Charles Spurgeon (1834–1892) lectured his ministerial candidates on this point:

> Of course, you are not such wiseacres as to think or say that you can expound Scripture without assistance from the works of divines and learned men who have laboured before you in the field of exposition. If you are of that opinion, pray remain so, for you are not worth the trouble of conversion…[and] would resent the attempt as an insult to your infallibility. It seems odd, that certain men who talk so much of what the Holy Spirit reveals to themselves, should think so little of what he has revealed to others.[11]

Scripture is given to the church as a whole, not to us as individuals. If, upon reading a particular passage, you have come up with an interpretation that has escaped the notice of every other Christian for two thousand years, or that has been championed by teachers the church deems heretical, the likelihood is pretty strong that you're wrong.

While Catholics believe that Sacred Scripture is a set of divinely revealed propositions, the Christian faith is not a "religion of the book" like Islam. It is rather a religion of the Word, which is, above all, incarnate and life-giving (see John 1:1–3, 14; Hebrews 4:12). It cannot be reduced to mere propositions or a dead letter. After all, the Son of God did not leave his eternal estate to give us a collection of manuscripts but, rather, to establish an ongoing community invested with his Holy Spirit, endowed with apostolic teaching authority and charged with transmitting his redemption to the world.

The Second Vatican Council summarized three broad criteria to help us rightly interpret Scripture according to the Spirit who inspired it (see *Dei verbum,* 12).

1. "Be especially attentive 'to the content and unity of the whole Scripture'" (*CCC,* #112). The Old Testament is the New concealed; the New Testament is the Old revealed. Scripture is a unity because God's plan is a coherent story with a divine author. "And beginning with Moses and all the prophets, he [the risen Christ] interpreted to them in all the scriptures the things concerning himself.... Then he said to them, 'These are my words which I spoke to you, while I was still with you, that everything written about me in the law of Moses and the prophets and the psalms must be fulfilled.' Then he opened their minds to understand the scriptures" (Luke 24:27, 44–45).

2. Scripture is to be read within "the living Tradition of the whole Church" (*CCC,* #112). The Bible is not private property. Rather it is given to guide a people. "All that has been said about interpreting Scripture is ultimately subject to the judgment of the Church which exercises

the divinely conferred commission and ministry of watching over and interpreting the Word of God" (*Dei verbum,* 12).

3.   Scripture illumines and is illuminated by the entire body of Christian truth and should be read in that light even as it gives light (see *CCC,* #114).

What is Scripture's relationship to Sacred Tradition?

Scripture is the written crystallization of Sacred Tradition. While it doesn't exhaust Sacred Tradition, we shouldn't imagine that Scripture is one thing and Sacred Tradition is something entirely different. In fact, the way we know what books constitute the library of Scripture is through Sacred Tradition.

We've all used an Etch-a-Sketch. Aluminum filings fill the screen, and by manipulating the knobs some of them can be made to form the written message: "We are aluminum filings." The written message and the materials out of which it is drawn are not one another. Nor does the written message reveal everything there is to know about the Etch-a-Sketch. Rather the written message focuses and communicates most explicitly the substance from which it derives.

Both Scripture and Tradition flow "from the same divine well-spring" and "come together in some fashion to form one thing, and move towards the same goal," which is the mystery of Christ. Together with Sacred Tradition, Scripture comprises "the supreme rule of [the church's] faith" (*Dei verbum,* 9, 21).

Sacred Tradition includes apostolic understandings not recorded in Scripture, so Christ's church "does not derive her certainty about all revealed truths from the holy Scriptures alone" (*CCC,* #82, quoting *Dei verbum,* 9). Jesus, his apostles and their successors pass along "the Way"—that is, a way of life, not merely a script or written propositions (see John 14:6; Acts 16:17; 18:25–26; 19:9, 23; 22:4; 24:14, 22; 2 Peter 2:2). Just as fathers and mothers teach their children far beyond what they say, so too does Mother Church. "Stand firm and hold fast to the traditions which you were taught by us, either by word of mouth or by letter" (2 Thessalonians 2:15). "You yourselves know how you ought to imitate us" (3:7).

This "Way" includes a wide range of beliefs, behaviors, ethical teachings, forms of prayer, liturgical gestures, ways of relating to one another and the outside world, all patterned and passed along by the apostles and their successors. "Be imitators of me.... Join in imitating me, and mark those who so live as you have an example in us," Paul wrote, thereby calling all believers to take note of his manner of life as well as his written words (1 Corinthians 4:16; Philippians 3:17).[12]

Many people mistakenly imagine that the New Testament is a charter document or a legislative text from which the church gains its legitimacy. The church is formed and sustained, rather, by the Incarnate Word, who reveals the will of God and passes his divine life and authority to the twelve. They in turn pass along that life-giving message to their successors, who expound and guard it (See Acts 20:28, 31; 1 Timothy 6:20; 2 Timothy 1:14). Catholics don't believe and practice things because they are in the Bible; they are in the Bible because the apostolic church taught and believed them. The New Testament is a "God-breathed" *witness* of that way of life; it is not the originator of it. "Sacred Tradition and sacred Scripture make up a single sacred deposit of the Word of God, which is entrusted to the Church.... But the task of giving an authentic interpretation of the Word of God, whether in its written form or in the form of Tradition, has been entrusted to the living teaching office of the Church alone" (*Dei verbum,* 10).[13]

Let me illustrate. Imagine that Henry Ford has set up an assembly plant in Dearborn, Michigan. There he trains workers to mass-produce cars. He is a very hands-on manager and oversees all aspects of the manufacturing process. He demonstrates how many rivets are needed, how to treat employees, when lunch breaks should occur, how to schedule shifts, how to perform customer service. He selects certain workers for more thorough training and establishes them as managers and superintendents to guarantee fidelity to his way of manufacturing.

After three years of intense instruction, Ford leaves to set up another plant in Wichita, Kansas. He shortly receives word that there is dissension and disarray at the Dearborn plant. Some are trying to alter his way of manufacturing. He writes a memo.

> Stand firm and hold fast to the traditions that you were taught. For three years I worked with you day and night that you might know the entire plan for auto assembly. Don't give a place to those who teach another way. Keep on doing what you have learned and received and heard and seen in me. Then you will have success. Let me remind you of some of the things I showed you.

He then summarizes a few key points. When the memo arrives, most of the workers say, "Yes, of course." But others try to use the brevity of the memo to claim that certain practices and instructions Ford had passed on while he was among them are now unnecessary, since he didn't specify them in the memo. Others counter, "Wait a minute. They aren't unnecessary. The memo just doesn't address them because he was focusing on the larger problem of staying faithful to the tradition he passed along to us. He didn't intend to re-teach us everything. Let's look to the men he trained as managers. They are the ones who knew him best."

The Ford workers don't believe and practice certain things about assembling cars because they are in the memo; they are in the memo because that is the way Ford workers had been instructed by Ford.

This roughly illustrates the relation between Tradition, Scripture and the bishops. The Gospels and epistles don't exhaust the tradition of the apostles but recall it and provide our most reliable documentation of it. From this witness of the New Testament we learn that the apostles passed along this "Way" and teaching authority to reliable men who were responsible for propagating, expounding and guarding the Sacred Tradition.

$\mathcal{W}$hy do Catholics put so much stock in the church fathers?

Just as the natural family rightly honors and gives great weight to the words of the father who gave it biological life, so too does the supernatural family of God revere those apostles, bishops and teachers who have transmitted the spiritual life that animates the church. The practice is taken from Scripture, where Abraham is called "our father" and "the father of all who believe" (Romans 4:12, 11; Acts 7:2). Paul is "a father in Christ Jesus through the gospel" (1 Corinthians 4:15) and calls the people he pastors "my children" (1 Thessalonians 2:11). John also encourages a filial devotion from his disciples by addressing them as "little children" (1 John 2:11), and Peter refers to "the fathers" who have fallen asleep (2 Peter 3:14).

Some try to argue from Matthew 23:8–12 that "no man is to be called father on earth for we have one Father, who is in heaven." Likewise, according to the same passage, we are to call no man "teacher" or "master." If the exaggeration in this passage is misconstrued as a literal command, then the above "paternal" passages are wickedly misleading, enticing us to do the very thing Christ forbids.

Furthermore, Saint Paul specifies that God the Holy Spirit has given "teachers" to the church just as he has given "apostles" and "prophets" and "workers of miracles" (see 1 Corinthians 12:28; Ephesians 4:11). The literalistic interpretation of Jesus' prohibition against calling anyone father or master or teacher on earth puts Saint Paul and other teachers in the silly position of modeling for us what Christ has forbidden.[14]

"Fathers of the church" is an affectionate and popular term rather than an exact title. Depending on whose list you are consulting, the fathers number about a hundred early Christian teachers. While most histories of the church focus on creeds and councils, persecutions and prefects, emperors and exiles, the church sees itself as a household of faith held together by strong fathers who strove to protect their spiritual children from danger, to discipline them and to teach them the Way of Jesus. These "fathers" also presided over the thanksgiving meal of the Eucharist and guarded the family's patrimony from thieves who tried to break in and steal.

The term *father* is not restricted to bishops or even to those of unimpeachable orthodoxy. The appeal to the "unanimous consent of fathers" as a collective of sound teachers whose authority was generally recognized began in the mid-fourth century. Within a century it was common to invoke "the fathers" as one of the authorities to settle disputes. This "unanimous consent of the fathers" is a moral consensus, not a uniformity of opinion or agreement without exception. Certain of the fathers may disagree on particular items of the faith.

They are a diverse lot, cut from very different cloth. While baptism immerses us into Christ and forms one mystical body, it does not impose one type of personality. Only an infinite number of personalities can image the infinite-personal God, so when God creates any one of us, he can afford to break the mold.

Jerome was as cantankerous as Martin of Tours was pacific. Origen was as speculative as John Chrysostom was practical. They were lawyers, rhetoricians, popes, hermits, slaves, Scripture scholars, celibates and fathers. They wrote in Latin, Greek, Syriac and Coptic and oftentimes approached preaching and theology with methods as strikingly different as those of John Paul II and your local fundamentalist evangelist.

The fathers were generally men of keen intellect, holiness and unswerving fidelity to the apostolic tradition. They could and did fight among one another, making the unity of the faith they exhibit a testimony to God's grace. Only God could hold them in one body.

The "Age of the Fathers" stretches from the last third of the first century until the death of John of Damascus in the East in 749 and the death of Gregory the Great in the West in 604, although some extend the latter to Isidore of Seville (d. 636) or even the Venerable Bede (d. 735).

"Patristics" is the academic field that studies them. Jacques-Paul Migne (1800–1875) published 162 volumes of the Greek (Eastern) and 221 of the Latin (Western) "fathers," called *Patrologia Graeca* and *Patrologia Latina* respectively. His work is still the standard means of reference and citation (abbreviated *PG* and *PL*) for most patristic authors, even though it has been supplemented and is gradually being replaced. We denote the fathers as Eastern or Western depending upon their cultural background, language and influence.

The church fathers are usually clustered into five classifications:

1. The *apostolic fathers* were the first generation of Christian teachers after the apostles.

2. The *apologists* gave themselves the task of making a reasoned defense of Christianity to the non-Christian world in the second and third centuries.

3. The *ante-Nicene fathers* flourished before the Christological controversies that led to the Council of Nicaea in 325.

4. The *Nicene fathers* guided us through the doctrinally turbulent fourth century, with its questions about the relationship between the Father and the Son.

5. The *post-Nicene Fathers* closed the patristic age, consolidated the teaching of Nicaea and worked through the post-Nicene councils. These latter two periods are often called the "Golden Age of the Fathers."[15]

The Apostolic Fathers

The apostolic fathers are those who taught with or in the shadow of the apostles. These include Clement of Rome, bishop and martyr; Ignatius of Antioch (35–107), bishop and martyr; Polycarp of Smyrna (65–155) and the second-century Christian slave Hermas, who wrote the visionary *Shepherd*. Some of these fathers' writings were revered as Scripture by certain local churches, although they lack the divinely revealed, creative insights of Paul, John or Hebrews and the mature and consistent exposition of the later fathers, like the Cappadocians and Augustine.

Reformed theologian Louis Berkhof summarizes a common observation: "It is frequently remarked that in passing from the study of the New Testament to that of the Apostolic Fathers one is conscious of a tremendous change. There is not the same freshness and originality, depth and clearness.... Moreover, it should be borne in mind that there were no philosophical minds among them with special training for the pursuit of the truth and outstanding ability for its systematic presentation."[16]

The Apologists and Ante-Nicene Fathers

The apologists (c. 120–220) are those fathers who shouldered the task of making a reasoned explanation of the faith when Christianity was first making significant inroads among the educated classes. They countered slanderous accusations, commonly hurled, which claimed Christians were cannibalistic, incestuous and atheistic. They tried to demonstrate that Christianity was no political threat to the emperors even though it offered a worldview superior to that of paganism.

The apologists include Justin Martyr (c. 100–165), who, when he refused to sacrifice, was convicted of impiety to the gods, then scourged and beheaded. His disciple Tatian (c. 150) produced a harmony of the Gospels and a scathing critique of Greek civilization. The best known of the apologists is the brilliant lawyer Tertullian (c. 160–225), whose hot head, quick love of ridicule and rigorism eventually landed him with a heretical sect called the Montanists. Some exclude him from the fathers because he died separated from the church he had devoted most of his life to serving. Also listed among the apologists are Aristides, Athenagoras, Theophilus and Minucius Felix.

The ante-Nicene fathers include Bishop Irenaeus of Lyons (c. 130–200), who knew Polycarp in his youth and whose theological writings became a watershed in the history of Christian thought. He is considered the first great Catholic theologian. At the age of forty-eight, showing great courage, he accepted ordination as bishop of Lyons after the martyrdom of his pred-ecessor. Whether or not he met a martyr's death is unclear.

Bishop and martyr Cyprian of Carthage (d. 258) forcefully argued that God's mercy must be extended to Christians who lapsed during the persecutions. During the terrible epidemic of 251 he urged his flock to serve Christian and non-Christian alike. For this he won great favor for the church among the watching pagan world. He came to be called the Father of Latin Theology and was beheaded for the faith.

Origen (c. 180–254), who saw his father die during the per-secutions, became the greatest teacher of Christian doctrine of his time. He is sometimes called the Father of Systematic Theology, having been philosophically trained in neo-Platonism. A prolific author, much of his work has been lost because his bold speculations led to condemnations and rejec-tion. In 250, under the persecution of Decius, he was impris-oned and tortured, and within a few years he died for his faith.

Clement of Alexandria (c. 150–215) was a philosopher, the-ologian and poet who tried to win the Gnostics to full faith in Christ by proposing a Christian "gnosis." His work, however, presupposes the Catholic faith.

The Nicene Fathers

In the fourth century the persecutions ended. The church was finally at peace with the empire. But as the external pressure of persecution receded, the internal pressure of theological division increased.

Arius of Alexandria began preaching the error that Jesus was not divine and coeternal with the Father. According to Arius and his followers, the Son of God was not God the Son but rather a creature. Arius claimed that there was a "time when the Son was not." The conflict that ensued gave rise to the Council of Nicea (A.D. 325) and later the "Golden Age of the Fathers."

Bishop and exile Athanasius of Alexandria (297–373) became the strongest defender of the Council of Nicaea. The council had used Athanasius' language that the Son was "one in being with the Father," true God of true God. The followers of Arius did not accept the results of the council and, with the support of various emperors, turned Athanasius' life into endless rounds of "fright, fight and flight." At one time it appeared that it was Athanasius against the world, from which has come the phrase "Athanasius *contra mundum*." Athanasius prevailed and spent the last seven years of his life peacefully in Alexandria. The Greek Orthodox church has rewarded Athanasius with the title "The Father of Orthodoxy."

Bishop Eusebius of Caesarea (263–340) is called the Father of Church History because his comprehensive *Ecclesiastical History* has shaped all future research into the history of Christianity. At the Council of Nicaea he proposed a middle way between Athanasius and Arius. His "solution" was rejected, and while he accepted the council's conclusion, he later aided in the harassment of Athanasius.

Other great Nicene fathers include the "Cappadocian Fathers": Basil the Great (the doer), who was an activist bishop and a thorn in the flesh of the Arian emperors; his brother Gregory of Nyssa (the thinker), the greatest speculative theologian of his time; and their longtime friend Gregory of Nazianzus (the dreamer), poet, preacher and bishop. Together they fought Arianism and laid the groundwork for the Council of Constantinople in 381, which hammered the final nail in the coffin of Arianism and gave us what we recite at Sunday Mass, "The Nicene Creed."

Bishop Cyril of Jerusalem (315–386) spent half of his forty years as a bishop exiled from his diocese during the Arian controversy. He is principally remembered today for his brilliant catechetical lectures to baptismal candidates.

Bishop Ambrose of Milan (340–397) was a Roman governor and prominent layman who went from baptism to bishop in eight days. "Perhaps no man played a greater part, in practice, in constructing the apparatus of practical belief which surrounded the European during the millennium when Christianity was the environment of society."[17]

Ambrose's greatest contribution as a father may be his part in the conversion of Saint Augustine, his most famous "son" in the faith. Oddly, from our perspective, Augustine is surprised that Ambrose read to himself, a habit unknown to the classical world: "His eyes scanned the page, and his mind penetrated its meaning, but his voice and tongue were silent."[18] Ambrose insisted that the emperor was not "above" the church but "within" it and thus subject to its discipline. By this teaching and the forceful steps he took to enforce it, he became the Father of Medieval Church-State Relations and a model of the princely bishop.

Post-Nicene Fathers

The years from the fifth to the eighth century saw the barbarian invasions, the collapse of the old Roman order and the rise of Islam. The church was not without fatherly guidance.

Jerome (342–420) was a man of extraordinary intellectual and literary gifts. In a dream he came under judgment for loving Cicero and classical literature more than Christian. Called the Father of Biblical Studies, his translation of the Bible from the original languages, known as the Latin Vulgate, became the standard of Western Christendom. His commentaries were unsurpassed in linguistic and geographical detail, as he had lived in Palestine among the Jews. He had a scholar's rather than an administrator's temperament, even though he managed to rule a monastery in Bethlehem, where he settled into the ascetic life of an agonized intellectual. He relished controversy and could be as sharp, even venomous, with his allies as with his enemies.

It can be said of Bishop Augustine of Hippo (354–430) that no other single Christian has more decisively shaped Western theology, philosophy, politics and psychology. His *City of God,* written while the barbarians were at the gates of his episcopal city of Carthage, argued that history was driven by the conflict between two competing social orders: one a city built on the pride of the natural man; the other the heavenly Jerusalem, built on the supernatural love of Christ through redeemed man.

Augustine's vision was expansive, far-reaching, strategic. Dry-eyed and clear minded, he watched as the emperor's use of force and his own use of the pulpit broke the back of the schismatic Donatists and reinforced both imperial and ecclesiastical cohesion. The Donatists had threatened that unity by refusing Communion to penitents who had lapsed during persecution. Augustine found this unthinkable for two reasons: First of all, the church was one in practice and holy in its purpose. The wheat and the tares, the good and the evil, would grow up together in the church, only to be separated at the Final Judgment. Further, the goal of human history was dawning with the universal spread of a culturally transformative Christianity.

With this as a backdrop, Augustine used rhetoric and ridicule to paint the Donatists as petty separatists: "The clouds roll with thunder, that the House of the Lord shall be built throughout the earth; and these frogs sit in their marsh and croak—'We are the only Christians!' "[19] He is sometimes called the Father of Psychology for the insightful introspection of the emotional or "affective" side of his religious experience in

Confessions. When the British theologian Pelagius attacked a sentence in it, a doctrinal controversy ensued over the nature of man, the Fall and grace.

John of Antioch (347–407) postponed a monastic call to care for his widowed mother. Later he damaged his health as a hermit. At age thirty-nine he was ordained a priest in Antioch, and reluctantly, he became a bishop twelve years later in Constantinople. In spite of his plain, even tactless preaching, he earned the nickname "Chrysostom," which means "golden-tongued," for his biblical homilies. Twice he was banished because of his preaching against the rich and powerful. He deplored fellow bishops who dressed like wealthy noblemen and ate sumptuously.

The love of his flock, and even the support of Pope Innocent I, couldn't secure John's protection from the elites whom he had offended. "He was exiled at first to near Antioch, and when it became clear that in spite of his enfeebled health, he would not die there soon enough, he was moved to Pontus, and finally deliberately killed by enforced traveling on foot in severe weather."[20]

When the Roman legal system, government and military finally buckled and collapsed, the church was the only intact social system remaining. Gregory the Great (540–604) called himself "an ape forced to play the lion."[21] He was the pope called upon to preside over the church's salvage effort by public preaching, encouraging people to repent and have hope. He initiated sweeping reforms of the clergy and the liturgy and increased social services through the network of the churches. He also strengthened the authority of the papacy, defended his bishops against secular rulers, arranged settlements and negotiated peace in the countrysides. To spread the faith he commissioned missionaries to distant places. His writings enormously influenced the Middle Ages and beyond.

The Catholic church honors eight as the "Great Fathers," four from the East and four from the West. Athanasius, Basil the Great, Gregory of Nazianzus and John Chrysostom are the Eastern Fathers. Ambrose of Milan, Augustine of Hippo, Jerome and Pope Gregory the Great are the Great Western Fathers.[22]

Who are the doctors of the church?

Doctor comes from the Latin *docere*, which simply means "to teach." After apostles and prophets, and before workers of miracles, Saint Paul lists "doctors" as Spirit-endowed gifts to the church (see 1 Corinthians 12:28).

Since all Christians are disciples—that is, learners (the Latin *discipulus* means "learner," from *discere*, "to learn")—one would expect teachers. We aren't cast into this buzzing, babbling world of confusion without resources. The God-seeker is an apprentice on the path to become a journeyman and eventually a master of the guild. Christ has provided teachers for his learners, his disciples. The faith is passed on and transmitted by others, not invented by the individual.

There have been many Christian teachers. Since the Middle Ages, however, the formal title of "doctor of the church" has been given to a relatively small number of teachers who possess special insight into the truths of the faith. The church honors them as models of instruction and sanctity.

These doctors of the church are not only extraordinary teachers but men and women of heroic virtue, all canonized saints. Their lives "adorned the doctrine" they taught, as Saint Paul instructed the pastor and teacher Titus: "Show yourself in all respects a model of good deeds, and in your teaching show integrity, gravity, and sound speech...[to all Christians] so that in everything they may adorn the doctrine of God our Savior" (Titus 2:7, 10).

Some doctors were exemplary teachers because of the way they lived. Nowhere is this so clearly illustrated as in the case of Saint Thérèse of Lisieux, whom Pope John Paul II declared a "doctor of the universal church" on World Mission Sunday, October 19, 1997. At the time of her death in 1897, this twenty-four-year-old Carmelite nun had never published a work of theology, never attended a university, never engaged in systematic study. And no one would have been as surprised as Thérèse Martin to find her playing in the same league as Saint Thomas Aquinas, Saint Augustine of Hippo, the great Cappodocians and her beloved Saint John of the Cross.

That an unlettered, twenty-four-year-old nun could become a saint is not surprising. That she could be declared a doctor of the church forces one to pause. But as John Paul II said in his proclamation: "During her life Thérèse discovered 'new lights, hidden and mysterious meanings'...and received from the divine Teacher that 'science of love' which she then expressed with particular originality in her writings.... It can be considered a special charism of Gospel wisdom which Thérèse, like other saints and teachers of faith, attained in prayer."[23]

All doctors of the church meet at least three criteria:

- ❖ eminent doctrine—that is, renowned for its conformity to Scripture and the Catholic faith;[24]

- ❖ outstanding holiness of life; and

- ❖ recognition by a pope or a legitimate general council.

Saint Thérèse clearly met these criteria, but further considerations were advanced. Even in the absence of a full body of doctrine, her "teaching" was currently as well as permanently relevant. Her writings amount to eight volumes including 266 letters, transcripts of last conversations, fifty-five poems, three manuscripts of her *Story of a Soul,* prayers and more.

Thérèse's life possesses a mystical quality that inspires others. Her autobiography, *Story of a Soul,* for instance, has been translated into fifty languages. What inspires people is her way of littleness, a way of trust and absolute surrender to God's intimate presence. She is able to communicate this through her life as a lived parable, truly the "story of a soul."

Pope John Paul II wrote:

> It must be said that Thérèse experienced divine revelation.... At the summit, as the source and goal, is the merciful love of the three Divine Persons.... At the root, on the subject's part, is the experience of being the Father's adoptive children in Jesus; this is the most authentic meaning of spiritual childhood, that is, the experience of divine filiation, under the movement of the Holy Spirit.... Through spiritual childhood one experiences that everything comes from God, returns to him and abides in him.... Such is the doctrinal message taught and lived by this Saint.[25]

So doctors of the church are not necessarily healers or workers of miracles or prophets. But they are teachers, by both precept and practice.

What is the relation between the fathers of the church and the doctors of the church? *Church father* is a popular term describing about a hundred teachers from the first eight centuries. *Doctor of the church* is a more formal title reserved for only thirty-three at the present time. Eight great fathers, four from the Western (Latin) church and four from the Eastern (Greek) church, are also considered doctors of the church.

They were formally recognized in 1298 and 1568, respectively. The Western great fathers are:

- ❖ Ambrose (c. 340–397), bishop of Milan, evangelist of Augustine

- ❖ Jerome (c. 343–420), the Father of Biblical Studies

- ❖ Augustine (354–430), the Doctor of Grace

- ❖ Gregory the Great (c. 540–604), reformer and defender of papal primacy

The Eastern great fathers are:

- ❖ Athanasius (c. 297–373), the Father of Orthodoxy

- ❖ Basil the Great (c. 329–379), the Father of Eastern Monasticism

- ❖ Gregory Nazianzen (c. 330–390), "the Christian Demosthenes"

- ❖ John Chrysostom (c. 347–407), the "Golden-Tongued" preacher

Here is a list of the other doctors, along with some description and the dates of their formal recognition by the church:

- ❖ Thomas Aquinas (1225–1274), Dominican, the Angelic Doctor, 1567

- ❖ Bonaventure (c. 1217–1274), Franciscan, the Seraphic Doctor, 1588

- ❖ Anselm (1033–1109), archbishop of Canterbury, the Father of Scholasticism, 1720

- ❖ Isidore of Seville (560–636), archbishop, the most learned man of his age, 1722

❖ Peter Chrysologus (c. 400–450), archbishop of Ravenna, the "Golden Speaker," 1729

❖ Leo I, the Great (400–461), the pope who saved Rome from Attila, 1754

❖ Peter Damian (1007–1072), Benedictine reformer, 1828

❖ Bernard of Clairvaux (1090–1153), Cistercian, the Mellifluous Doctor, 1830

❖ Hilary of Poitiers (c. 315–368), bishop, the "Athanasius of the West," 1851

❖ Alphonsus Liguori (1696–1787), founder of the Redemptorists, perhaps the greatest moralist, 1871

❖ Francis de Sales (1567–1622), bishop, leader of the Catholic Reformation, expert on the devotional life, 1877

❖ Cyril of Alexandria (c. 376–444), patriarch who presided over the Council of Ephesus, 1882

❖ Cyril of Jerusalem (c. 315–387), the great bishop-catechist, Eastern opponent of Arianism, 1882

❖ John Damascene (675–749), monk, defender of sacred icons, 1890

❖ Bede the Venerable (c. 673–735), Benedictine priest, Father of English History, 1899

❖ Ephraem of Syria (c. 306–373), deacon of Edessa, the "Harp of the Holy Spirit," 1920

❖ Peter Canisius (1521–1597), Jesuit theologian, leader of the Catholic Reformation, 1925

❖ John of the Cross (1542–1591), cofounder of the Discalced Carmelites, the Doctor of Mystical Theology, 1926

❖ Robert Bellarmine (1542–1621), Jesuit, reformer and canonist, 1931

❖ Albert the Great (c. 1200–1280), Dominican, the Universal Doctor, 1931

❖ Anthony of Padua (1195–1231), Franciscan friar, the Evangelical Doctor, 1946

❖ Lawrence of Brindisi (1559–1619), Capuchin, the leading preacher in the Catholic Reformation, 1959

❖ Teresa of Avila (1515–1582), the mystical Carmelite, 1970

❖ Catherine of Siena (c. 1347–1380), who promoted the end of the Avignon papacy, mystic, 1970

❖ Thérèse of Lisieux (1873–1897), Carmelite, the Little Flower, 1997

How do Catholics view the other religions of the world?

Since all human beings are created in the image and likeness of God, they are made for God. Saint Augustine said that our hearts are restless until they find their rest in him.[26]

Human existence, indeed, raises many riddles. Who are we? Where are we? Why is there suffering, unhappiness, frustration? How do we find healing, happiness, holiness? What is our relation to ultimate reality? Is there life after death? What constitutes the good, the true and the beautiful?

Throughout history human beings have sought answers to these questions. Many of the answers proffered and accepted through the centuries form the complex religious history of humanity, including the major religious traditions of Hinduism, Buddhism, Islam, Judaism and Christianity. "All men form but one community. This is so because all stem from the one stock which God created to people the entire earth (cf. Acts 17:26), and also because all share a common destiny, namely God" (*Nostra aetate,* 1).[27]

The Catholic church believes that all truth is God's truth, and so the church "rejects nothing of what is true and holy in these religions. She has a high regard for the manner of life and conduct, the precepts and doctrines which, although differing in many ways from her own teaching, nevertheless often reflect a ray of that truth which enlightens all men" (*Nostra aetate,* 2).[28]

Respect and dialogue, however, are not incompatible with proclamation and mission. The church is duty-bound to proclaim without fail Christ who is "the way, the truth and the life" (John 14:6). "In Christ God was reconciling the world to himself, not counting their trespasses against them, and entrusting the message of reconciliation to us. So we are ambassadors for Christ" (2 Corinthians 5:19–20).

The Christian story can be thought of as four chapters: creation, fall, redemption and consummation. Or put more simply: God created; man fell; Jesus redeemed; he's coming again to finish the job. It might be helpful to look at these four chapters in light of this question.

Creation: All human beings are created in the image and likeness of God and can only fulfill their nature by union with him and his will. This, of course, includes Hindus, Muslims, animists and so on.

Fall: All human beings form consciences, ask questions, hunger for meaning and God. Being separated from God by sin, however, they grope along, fashioning answers that conform more or less to the truth. Because of this rupture with God and others, falsehood enters the world of religions.

Redemption: Christ died for all human beings, and all human beings can share in that redemption. Only God is able to judge who will be saved. Christ established his church as the vehicle to proclaim this good news.

Consummation: Christ will return publicly, and every knee shall bow, gratefully or begrudgingly, and every tongue confess that Jesus Christ is Lord to the glory of God the Father (see Philippians 2:10–11).

To believe that Christ is God in human flesh and that his body, the church, is bound to declare these truths to the world is not institutional pride or chauvinism but rather a matter of fidelity. Most other religions are based on a set of practices or a body of teachings; Christianity is based on the identity and person of its founder. The New Testament presents Jesus as the definitive and final revelation of God until the end of history.

Jesus is the victor over death and the liberator from sin. Simple fidelity to the New Testament requires Christians to present Jesus as the Lord and Savior of the world, even while acknowledging that other world religions embody certain truths. Socrates asked, "What is truth?" Buddha taught the four noble truths, Mohammed claimed to receive the truth, the apostles bore witness to the truth, but only Jesus dared to say, "I am…the truth…; no one comes to the Father, but by me" (John 14:6). You might say he made it personal. This was the proclamation of the apostolic church: "There is salvation in no one else, for there is no other name under heaven given among men by which we must be saved" (Acts 4:12).

Christ and his closest followers saw him as the Lord of creation and redemption, not just another religious leader. To fail to follow their example would make today's Christians unfaithful witnesses to their most primitive creed: "Jesus is Lord" (1 Corinthians 12:3).

The Jews

"Salvation is from the Jews," Jesus told the Samaritan woman at the well (John 4:22). The Catholic church is deeply linked to the Jewish people, who were "'the first to hear the Word of God.' The Jewish faith, unlike other non-Christian religions, is already a response to God's revelation" (*CCC*, #839).[29] And "the gifts and the call of God are irrevocable" (Romans 11:29). We share a common spiritual heritage. To the Jews, Paul writes, "belong the sonship, the glory, the covenants, the giving of the law, the worship, and the promises; to them belong the patriarchs, and of their race, according to the flesh, is the Christ" (Romans 9:4–5).

Jesus, Mary, Joseph and the apostles were all Jews. All but one of the New Testament authors were Jews. Virtually all the earliest disciples of Jesus were Jews. Does the obvious need to be said? Jesus was a Jew, and Christianity is Jewish.

Both Catholics and the Jewish people await the Messiah. Catholics await his Second Coming; the Jewish people await "the coming of a Messiah, whose features remain hidden till the end of time" (*CCC*, #840). The Jewish people have not accepted, known or understood Christ Jesus as this Messiah. "The glorious Messiah's coming is suspended at every moment of history until his recognition by 'all Israel.'... The 'full inclusion' of the Jews in the Messiah's salvation, in the wake of 'the full number of the Gentiles,' will enable the People of God to achieve 'the measure of the stature of the fullness of Christ,' in which 'God may be all in all'" (*CCC*, #674).[30]

While certain Jewish authorities pressed Roman authorities

for the death of Jesus, neither all Jews at that time nor through-out history are culpable for his death, any more than any other members of the human race for whom Christ died.

Muslims

> The Church has also a high regard for the Muslims. They worship God, who is one, living and subsistent, merciful and almighty, the Creator of heaven and earth, who has also spoken to men. They strive to submit themselves without reserve to the hidden decrees of God, just as Abraham submitted himself to God's plan, to whose faith Muslims eagerly link their own. Although not acknowledging him as God, they venerate Jesus as a prophet, his virgin Mother they also honor, and even at times devoutly invoke. Further, they await the day of judgment and the reward of God following the resurrection of the dead. For this reason they highly esteem an upright life and worship God, especially by way of prayer, alms-deeds and fasting.
>
> Over the centuries many quarrels and dissensions have arisen between Christians and Muslims. The sacred Council now pleads with all to forget the past, and urges that a sincere effort be made to achieve mutual understanding; for the benefit of all men, let them together preserve and promote peace, liberty, social justice and moral values. (*Nostra Aetate,* 3)

I quote the entire passage on the Muslims from Vatican II rather than the abbreviated version in the *Catechism* (#841) because the differences between Islam and Christianity are so profound that people of good will could easily despair of meaningful conversation. It may be significant that the church does not in this passage refer to Islam as a "religion" but to Muslims as religious men and women with particular beliefs.

For Muslims the supreme revelation is the Koran, a book of 114 chapters or Suras. Oftentimes people make the mistake of thinking that when comparing Christianity and Islam, the Koran is roughly equivalent to the Bible. On the surface it simply appears that Muslims have a holy book and Christians have a holy book. But this is a false equivalence. For Muslims the supreme revelation of God is inscripturated in the Koran. For Christians the supreme revelation is incarnated in Jesus Christ. Muslims are a people of the book; Christians are a people of the Word made flesh.

The koranic portrait of Jesus includes his virgin birth, his role as a prophet, his mission to confirm the Torah but to set aside some of its prohibitions, his calling of "helpers" in his mission. Though Muslims respect Jesus as a spiritual teacher (Ibn 'Arabi [d. 1240] even called Jesus "the seal of holiness"), they also regard as blasphemous the Christian teaching that God took on human flesh. They deny the triune God, the deity of Christ and the personality of the Holy Spirit. Muslims also believe that the Old and New Testaments are unreliable records that have been deliberately corrupted.

No Christian who seeks to be a faithful witness can acquiesce to the belief that all religions are essentially the same. Nakedly put, if Christianity is true, Islam must be false, although God may honor the personal faith of particular Muslims. No earnest Muslim would disagree. Respect for Christ and Muslims requires this candor.[31]

Naturally, Catholics welcome opportunities to work together with Muslims or any person of goodwill to support human dignity, alleviate injustice, oppose moral evils or partner in the arts and sciences. For example, in 1995 the American Muslim Council gave Cardinal William Keeler the Mahmoud Abu Saud Excellence Award. In his acceptance speech the cardinal urged Muslims and Catholics to work together to promote "a restoration of basic moral teaching in the public schools," oppose all forms of pornography, "especially that directed at children," and approach media leaders and advertisers "regarding immorality and violence in the media."

Noting that the interfaith banquet was held on the Feast of the Immaculate Conception, the cardinal said: "Catholics are delighted to learn that there are more verses in the Qur'an—thirty-four of them—which name the Blessed Virgin Mary than there are in the whole New Testament." He said that while Muslims do not believe that Mary is the mother of God, they hold her in great esteem. Keeler said that although a "radical difference in faith forever separates us" with regard to Mary, "it paradoxically also holds us forever in conversation with one another."[32]

Hindus

In Hinduism "men explore the divine mystery and express it both in the limitless riches of myth and the accurately defined insights of philosophy. They seek release from the trials of the present life by ascetical practices, profound meditation and recourse to God in confidence and love" (*Nostra aetate,* 2).

"Many Hindus have no difficulty in accepting Jesus as divine." They worship various deities at various shrines. What they cannot accept is "that the Incarnation of God in Jesus is unique. Jesus is often seen as the supreme example of self-realization, the goal of the Hindi dharma.... According to Hindu traditions, history always provides an imperfect knowledge of reality. In such a context, to identify the mystery of Jesus Christ with historical fact is seen as reducing God to imperfection."[33]

Mother Teresa's corporal works of mercy bore witness to the love of Christ for the Hindu people. The phenomenal display of affection upon her death is instructive.

Buddhists

"Buddhism in its various forms testifies to the essential inadequacy of this changing world. It proposes a way of life by which men can, with confidence and trust, attain a state of perfect liberation and reach supreme illumination either through their own efforts or by the aid of divine help" (*Nostra aetate,* 2).

Buddhism does offer, like Christianity, a way of salvation. But Buddhism proposes a salvation not from sin but from the world, which is a metaphysical deliverance rather than a moral transformation. In Buddhism the world itself is the source of evil and suffering. Pope John Paul II explained the Buddhist response: "To liberate oneself from this evil, one must free oneself from this world, necessitating a break with the ties that join us to external reality—ties existing in our human nature, in our psyche, in our bodies."[34]

The end result is a detachment, even an indifference to what is in the world, including fellow creatures. Recipients of Buddhist "enlightenment" do not perfect their natures in loving union with the Creator; they enter a state of perfect nothingness, *nirvana.*

From a Christian standpoint, the world was created "good" by a wise, loving, personal God. Sin, not the world, is to be escaped. While the detachment from the world sought in Buddhism bears some similarities with the Christian mystics of northern Europe, like Meister Eckhart or the later Carmelite mystics like Teresa of Avila, the Christian mystics do not see detachment as an end in and of itself.

"[Saint John of the Cross] proposes detachment from the world in order to unite oneself to that which is outside of the world—by this I do not mean nirvana, but a personal God. Union with Him comes about not only through purification, but through love. *Carmelite mysticism begins at the point where the reflections of Buddha end.*"[35]

Nevertheless, Catholics respect and maintain dialogue with Buddhists, searching for common ground in the human quest for salvation. In July 1996 Buddhist and Christian monks met at the Abbey of Gethsemani in Kentucky to discuss ultimate reality, spirituality, worship, tragedy, violence, mind, virtue, grace and social action.[36] The Congregation for the Doctrine of the Faith has noted, however, that "proposals to harmonize Christian meditation with eastern techniques need to have their contents and methods ever subjected to a thorough-going examination so as to avoid the danger of falling into syncretism."[37]

The Catholic church understands the spirit of tolerance that may lead some people to believe that all religions are essentially one. But such is a false and dangerous position. God the Son, who took on human flesh in the womb of Mary, worked wonders, died for the sins of the world and rose from the dead, ascended to heaven, sending the Holy Spirit to constitute his church and make him available in both Word and sacrament, is not just one avatar or guru or prophet or good teacher. He is the eternal Word draped in human nature.

> With the coming of the Saviour Jesus Christ, God has willed that the Church founded by him be the instrument for the salvation of all humanity. This truth of faith does not lessen the sincere respect which the Church has for the religions of the world, but at the same time, it rules out, in a radical way, that mentality of indifferentism "characterized by a religious relativism which leads to the belief that 'one religion is as good as another'" (*Dominus Iesus,* 22).[38]

Similarly, the Catholic church believes that "countless people throughout the centuries have been and still are able today to nourish and maintain their life-relationship with God" through non-Christian sacred texts, such as the Koran and Hinduism's

Bhagavad Gita and Upanishads. "The Church's tradition, how-ever, reserves the designation of *inspired texts* to the canonical books of the Old and New Testaments, since these are inspired by the Holy Spirit" (*Dominus Iesus,* 8). God is the author of the Bible in a way that these other texts do not and cannot claim (see John 20:31; 2 Timothy 3:16; 2 Peter 1:19–21; 3:15–16).

People are of equal worth; religious claims are not.

Do Catholics believe non-Christians can be saved?

The Catholic church recognizes that God is free to save whomever he wishes. But whoever is redeemed and brought into union with God is done so, objectively speaking, through the work of Christ. In other words, Christ is the Savior, the one mediator between God and man. Even if people haven't yet heard the gospel proclamation that "dying he destroyed our death, rising he restored our life," they can be united to God. This may appear contradictory; it is not.

All human beings have a duty to embrace the light they receive—that is, the light that enlightens every man who comes into the world (John 1:9). That light is Christ. All human beings have a duty to respond to the truth as they know it. That truth is Christ. For example, Saint Paul argued that the non-Jews who had not received the Torah—the Jewish Law—would be judged apart from the law and according to the law on their hearts.

> All who have sinned without the law will also perish without the law, and all who have sinned under the law will be judged by the law. For it is not the hearers of the law who are righteous before God, but the doers of the law who will be justified. When Gentiles who have not the law do by nature what the law requires, they are a law to themselves, even though they do not have the law. They show

that what the law requires is written on their hearts, while their conscience also bears witness and their conflicting thoughts accuse or perhaps excuse them on that day when, according to my gospel, God judges the secrets of men by Christ Jesus. (Romans 2:12–16)

People cannot be held responsible for what they don't know. In Catholic thought this is called "invincible ignorance."

On the other hand, all people have, by virtue of their creation, some interior revelation of God to which they are bound to respond positively if they are to live in fellowship with their Creator. By responding to Christ to the degree that they apprehend him, Christ can redeem them. "Those who, through no fault of their own, do not know the Gospel of Christ or his Church, but who nevertheless seek God with a sincere heart, and, moved by grace, try in their actions to do his will as they know it through the dictates of their conscience—those too may achieve eternal salvation" (*Lumen gentium,* 16).[39]

So will non-Christians be saved? In the abstract I answer yes. In the concrete I answer, I don't know any who will just as I don't know any who won't be saved.

As Paul lays out frightfully in Romans 1:18–25, human beings can become vain in their reasonings and exchange the truth of God for a lie. They can lapse into despair because of toxic religion and false beliefs that are influenced by the evil one. The Congregation for the Doctrine of the Faith stated, "Some prayers and rituals of the other religions may assume a role of preparation for the Gospel.... One cannot attribute to these, however, a divine origin.... Furthermore, it cannot be overlooked that other rituals, insofar as they depend on superstitions or other errors, constitute an obstacle to salvation" (*Dominus Iesus,* 21).

While it is possible for those who haven't heard the gospel to be reconciled with God, yet we greatly enhance their prospects by going into all the world with the Word of Christ. We have a missionary mandate to present the gospel of God's love in a way that peels away the distortions that have grown up like barnacles on the religious consciousness of mankind. The gospel refocuses mankind's native religious awareness; it republishes the general revelation for which people grope in nature. It brings sight to the eyes, healing to the body, strength to the weak, freedom to the captive.

It is worth noting that immediately after the *Catechism*'s discussion of non-Christian religions, it moves to the church's missionary mandate (see *CCC*, #849–856). Part of that includes: "The ultimate purpose of mission is none other than to make men share in the communion between the Father and the Son in their Spirit of love" (*CCC*, #850).

How should I respond to claims of apparitions?

Claims of supernatural revelation abound. The good news is that there are many guidelines to help those interested sort through the various claims of visions and apparitions. Dreams, visions, revelations, apparitions (appearances) are part and parcel of biblical spirituality. Throughout human history, people have claimed visitations from the divine, and Scripture records many and diverse apparitions.[40]

Divine revelation climaxed when God himself took on human nature and disclosed himself as tangibly as anybody could expect (see John 1:1–14; Colossians 2:9; Hebrews 1:1–2). The Incarnation capped off what is called "public revelation"— that is, revelation that all Christians must receive as authoritative.

God, however, continues to disclose himself and guide us

through dreams, visions, apparitions of his saints and so on. These "private" revelations do not convey new information about God and his plan. They don't add anything to the deposit of faith the church received from Christ and the apostles. They don't change anything in Catholic doctrine. In fact, with the exception of the visions of the resurrected Christ, the church doesn't even teach as fact that Christ or Mary or the archangel Michael appeared to this mystic or that, at this particular day and hour, and logged in with a particular message.

The Catholic church doesn't require belief in any apparitions except those in Scripture. Even apparitions considered "worthy of belief" aren't necessary for salvation. Rather, private revelations have a pastoral intent—that is, they help us to live "Christ's definitive revelation…more fully…in a certain period of history" (*CCC, #67*).

"Private" revelations apply "public" revelation. Just as sermons and homilies apply and illustrate Scripture, so too do apparitions apply and illustrate revealed doctrine. They spotlight and hone in on some particular aspect of Sacred Tradition, reemphasize it, urge us to act on it and motivate us to reconsider truths we may have neglected. Let me lay out my list of guidelines for dealing with claims of supernatural revelations.

1. First of all, I thank God that I live in a universe open to God and supernatural influence. Reality isn't hemmed in by the suffocating limits of materialism. Bertrand Russell was wrong when he lamented in his autobiography: "We stand on the shore of an ocean, crying to the night, and in the emptiness sometimes a voice answers out of the darkness. But it is the voice of one drowning, and in a moment the silence returns."[41]

Revelation assures me that I, a self-conscious, rational creature, am not alone in the universe. When I say, "Thank you," there is Someone who can say, "You're welcome." God is there, and he is not silent. So I start with thanksgiving for the infinite, personal God and my sense of place and call in this world.

2. I then ask: Does this claimed revelation contradict the Word of God contained in Scripture and Sacred Tradition? Happily, this test eliminates the vast majority of candidates. For instance, Christians might respect Mohammed's crusade against the polytheism that infected the tribes of the Arabian Peninsula during his lifetime (c. 570–629).

   But when he claims that Allah denies Christ's divinity, we know we are dealing with a false revelation.

   The late Edna Ballard (1886–1971) claimed to receive Ascended Master dictations or discourses from the seventh sphere of consciousness. These Ascended Masters revealed that the crucifixion was a victory of the sinister force, could not be considered redemptive and shouldn't be meditated upon or visualized. I don't hesitate to call her a false prophet.

   My most basic question is: Does the "new" revelation square with the "old" revelation?

3. I don't allow myself to get bullied by either the cheerleaders or the mockers of the apparition. Breathless excitement or simmering scorn is not discernment. Both can lead to rash judgments. Listen to the champions and the critics, and prayerfully evaluate their evidence. Respectful levelheadedness, not juvenile enthusiasm or cynical derision, best insures authentic discernment.

4. I try to be judicious, rather than petty, and focus on the overall thrust of the message. Private revelation hasn't the inspiration and inerrancy of Scripture. Margaret Mary Alacoque, whose revelation of the Sacred Heart has adorned and titled our hospitals, parishes and schools, admitted that she failed to perfectly transmit the message. Saints John of the Cross, Bernadette of Lourdes, Catherine of Siena and Teresa of Avila all confessed to the fallibility of their reporting. Saint John of the Cross concluded: "It is clear that, although sayings and revelations may be of God, we cannot always have confidence in them, for we can very easily be greatly deceived by them because of our manner of understanding them."[42] So don't get too picky about the details.

5. Is the revelation mediated to the seer by suspect means? "All forms of divination are to be rejected.... Consulting horoscopes, astrology, palm reading, interpretation of omens and lots, the phenomena of clairvoyance, and recourse to mediums all conceal a desire for power over time, history, and, in the last analysis, other human beings" (*CCC*, #2116).

As a rule of thumb, I regard activities normally associated with the occult as fraudulent, false or diabolical. Such activities are usually marked by the use of some "technique" to tap into hidden power. Phenomena originating with the grace of God cannot be manipulated by meditation exercises, ritual magic, Tarot cards, psychdelic drugs, ouija boards and so on.

Saint Teresa of Avila, who had no lack of visions, warns against even petitioning God for private revelations, never mind employing techniques to generate them. "I will only warn you that, when you learn or hear that God is granting souls these graces, you must never beg or desire Him to lead you by this road. Even if you think it is a very good one…there are certain reasons why such a course is not wise." Her reasons include lack of humility, demonic vulnerability, danger of auto-suggestion, likelihood of presumption and the heavy trials that come with such experiences.[43]

6. I learn what I can of the moral and spiritual life of the seer. Of course, if the seer is already canonized, his or her heroic virtue is settled although the content of the messages is not. Do the messages sound like unresolved personal grievances writ large on an alleged supernatural billboard for all to see?

Pay special attention to the attitudes of the seer. Does he or she exhibit pride, arrogance, ostentatious piety, greed or ungodly ambition? As early as the *Didache,* Christians were warned against itinerant prophets and apostles who stayed longer than two days and asked for money. "Not every one who speaks in the Spirit is a prophet; but only if he holds the ways of the Lord. Therefore from their ways shall the false prophet and the prophet be known."[44]

While the allure of dreams, visions and revelations proves enchanting to many, the truth is that most people attain holiness without private revelation. It's worth noting that neither Saint Thérèse of Lisieux nor Saint Maximillian Kolbe experienced private revelation.

And many who claim private revelation are not holy. Jesus spoke some dreadful words to this point:

> Not every one who says to me, "Lord, Lord," shall enter the kingdom of heaven, but he who does the will of my Father who is in heaven. On that day many will say to me, "Lord,

Lord, did we not prophesy in your name, and cast out demons in your name, and do many mighty works in your name?" And then will I declare to them, "I never knew you; depart from me, you evildoers." (Matthew 7:21–23)

7. I examine the spiritual and practical impact of the phenomenon on the lives of those enthused by it. Saint Paul's command is especially valuable in these situations: "Do not quench the Spirit, do not despise prophesying, but test everything: hold fast to what is good" (1 Thessalonians 5:19–21).

I taste the spiritual fruit of the message and movement. Are the messages filled with fear, rancor or bitterness? Are they bringing forth fruit unto repentance? Is the phenomenon leading me to deeper conversion? Am I sacrificing more? Sharing my faith? Excited about Scripture and the sacraments? Enthusiastic about worship? Overcoming temptation? Willing to embrace suffering?

Are there physical healings or other signs and wonders? The church's demand for proof in these matters is very high. At Lourdes, after thousands of apparent miracles, the church has accepted only a little more than sixty cases as authentic.

Do I understand the words of Saint Thérèse of Lisieux: "To ecstasy, I prefer the monotony of sacrifice"?[45] Do the apparition, the seer and the climate created by the phenomenon lead me to more fully love and obey Christ?

Authentic apparitions reflect the priorities of the Mother of God when she commanded the wine stewards at Cana of Galilee, "Do whatever [Jesus] tells you" (John 2:5). Are those claiming a special work of the Holy Spirit doing what the Spirit came to do?

Jesus said, "When the Counselor comes…even the Spirit of truth…he will bear witness to me; and you also are witnesses" (John 15:26–27). Is the focus on Jesus or on the intrigue of the paramystical phenomenon itself? Good trees bring forth good fruit (see Matthew 7:15–20).

8. I keep the whole phenomenon in perspective. At best it is a helpful grace, but it has no authority to demand my acceptance. I am free to exercise prudence and ignore the claim in order to get on with other spiritual priorities. Pope Benedict XIV said:

> What is to be said of those private revelations which the Apostolic See has *approved* of, those of the Blessed Hildegard (which were approved in part by Eugene III), of St. Bridget [by Boniface IX], and of St. Catherine of Siena [by Gregory XI]? We have already said that those revelations, although approved of, ought not to, and cannot, receive from us any assent of Catholic, but only of human faith, according to the rules of prudence, according to which the aforesaid revelations are probable, and piously to be believed.[46]

Remember that ultimately the decision to approve or disapprove the phenomenon is not yours. The church has either ignored it, approved it or disproved it or is investigating it. I can pursue it accordingly, but I am not the arbiter of truth in this matter. So I relax and enjoy the grace of God.

Part II

Salvation and Sacraments

*A*re Catholics "saved"?

It all depends on what one means by "saved." It's a little like the question "Are students learned?" Salvation, like learning, is a process. Students are learning and will be learned if they continue to be instructed. They certainly are more learned than they were before they began learning. But they are not yet learned in the final sense of the word. So it is with the question "Are Catholics saved?" Catholics are "saved" to the degree that they have cooperated with the grace of God offered to them as a free gift in Christ Jesus.

But this doesn't often satisfy those who ask the question, because they usually assume that salvation is complete at the moment one exercises faith in Christ. Once the sinner has turned to Christ, he is eternally secure, they say; heaven is guaranteed. "Salvation," in this sense, means a once-for-all completed act that cannot be undone. While not all evangelical or fundamentalist Protestants believe this, the ones most likely to ask the above question usually do.

A simple way to test this definition of salvation is to ask, "How does Scripture describe 'saved' people?" If we patiently catalogue all the relevant verses, we learn that salvation has a past, present and future dimension. So when asked, "Kresta, are you saved?" I answer:

"Yes, by the grace of God, *I have been* saved according to 2 Timothy 1:9; Titus 3:5; Romans 8:24 and Ephesians 2:5–8.

"And yes, by the grace of God, *I am presently in the process* of working out my salvation according to Philippians 2:12; 1 Corinthians 1:18; 15:2 and Acts 2:47.

"And yes, if I continue in the grace of God, *I will in the future* be saved according to Matthew 24:13; Romans 5:9–10; 13:11; 1 Corinthians 3:12–15; 1 Timothy 4:16 and Hebrews 9:28.

"Thank you for your concern. By the way, what do *you* mean by *salvation?*"

As a young boy I hit a line-drive homer into Mrs. Wright's living room, shattering her picture window. While she was quick to forgive, replacing the window was another matter. What was broken needed to be restored before I was fully "saved" from her "wrath." She didn't leave me on my own but offered me light employment in her apple orchard and back-yard, bringing me lunch and conversation, until I could earn enough to replace the window. I was glad to cooperate.

Salvation is more than God's initial forgiveness of the repen-tant sinner. Salvation is the work of God by which he is sal-vaging his broken creation and healing our sin-sick souls. When we repent of our sin and are baptized, we receive God's Spirit and the free gift of forgiveness purchased for us by Christ's atoning, sacrificial death (see Acts 2:38; Romans 3:22–26; 6:3–4). We are born again and begin our lives as chil-dren of God (see John 3:5), striving to imitate Christ, our elder brother, and growing in love and holiness unto full maturity (see Matthew 5:48; Ephesians 4:12–16; 1 Peter 1:15–16).

It is perfectly appropriate to say along our path of redemp-tion, "I am saved," as long as we aren't denying our ongoing need to cooperate with God's grace. Salvation is a progressive work of transformation and restoration that won't reach com-pletion until we stand before God and behold him face-to-face in what Catholics call "the beatific vision."

Sometimes a person will say, "What do you mean, salvation is a process? You are either saved or you are not! Look at the thief on the cross (Luke 23:43) or the Philippian jailer (Acts 16:31). There was no process there, no inner rehabilitation.

When the jailer cried, 'What must I do to be saved?' Paul and Silas replied, 'Believe on the Lord Jesus, and you will be saved.'"

Indeed, when I meet a person on his deathbed, as in the case of the thief on the cross or a person who fears dying in an earthquake as did the Philippian jailer, I am prepared to give him the "emergency gospel." A one-liner will do just fine under the circumstances. God will meet people where they are in order to bring them to where he is. But both situations are abnormal, and we would be ignoring hundreds of other passages of Scripture if we elevated these crisis presentations as the norm of gospel preaching.

Human sin has ruptured our relationship with God, shattered the unity of the human race, divided our psyche and even ravaged our nature. This mess can't just be forgiven or excused; it must be cleaned up. At God's invitation we become his workmanship and his coworkers in this reclamation effort, as we labor to become conformed to the image of Christ. "He who does not take his cross and follow me is not worthy of me" (Matthew 10:38; see also 1 Corinthians 3:9; Ephesians 2:10).

So we are saved inasmuch as we have entered Christ's way of redemption through faith and baptism. We are being saved inasmuch as God is presently at work within us, repairing the damage sin has caused. We will be saved inasmuch as the great and final day of the Lord will unveil a new creation unmarred by human sin, and perfect union will be reestablished between God and his creation.

Why do Catholics do penance, if Jesus has forgiven them?

We must become coworkers with God in restoring the fallen world that we deformed by our sin. At Calvary Jesus accomplished all that was necessary for our redemption. But the Holy Spirit must still apply his redemption to our lives. In this we have a share and must cooperate. Or as Saint Paul, the apostle of grace, put it without in any way belittling the finished work of Christ: "In my flesh I complete what is lacking in Christ's afflictions" (Colossians 1:24; see Philippians 3:10–11; 1 Corinthians 3:9; 2 Corinthians 6:1; 1 Thessalonians 3:2).

Penance recognizes that sin not only needs to be forgiven but that the damage sin causes to our inner selves and our neighbors needs to be repaired. Every sin disturbs the spiritual equilibrium of the universe. Even our most private sins affect our relationship with not only God but other men and women. For example, our resentment against a coworker manifests itself in a cold handshake and then returns to us through the grapevine in bitter words about our impersonal management style. Our lust for a neighbor lingers in a too-long glance and returns to us in a dinner invitation that tests our chastity.

Though anger and murder, lust and adultery, are not of equal gravity, Jesus knows that all create moral mayhem in our relational universe. People who understand the grace of God don't go around just saying they are sorry. They want to make wrong words right, straighten crooked roads, unbend everything they have twisted.

Some will argue that works of penance make void the sacrifice of Christ. If Jesus did it all, then why do penance? The answer is simple: redemption includes not only forgiveness but healing.

Sin bears two consequences, the eternal and the temporal. First, sin separates us from the eternal God. The consequence is *eternal:* hell. Confession, faith, repentance and its fruits can avoid such an end (see Acts 2:38; Romans 10:9; James 2:14–17; 1 John 1:9). Throughout our lives God woos us, calling us into union with him. He sends his Son to die on our behalf and communicates the lengths to which he will go to redeem us. If at the end of our lives we haven't responded, then he says to us: "You have refused me throughout time. Now you enter eternity just as you are, without a relationship with me. All your life you have said, 'My will be done,' rather than, 'Thy will be done.' I now grant that wish. You will live forever apart from me."

Penance, on the other hand, seeks to alleviate the *temporal* consequences of sin. Sin breaks our relationship with others. If we steal money from our neighbor, we must not only repent and seek forgiveness but also return the money. Zaccheus, for instance, returned it fourfold (see Luke 19:8–9). He looked up those who had been harmed by his sin, sought their forgiveness and made restitution.

Sin also affects our inner life. It bends our will in the direction of evil. Grace-filled good works bend it back in the direction of God. In the movie *The Mission,* Robert De Niro plays a proud slaver who kills his brother in a fit of rage. In prison a Jesuit priest, played by Jeremy Irons, befriends him. He repents and joins the Jesuits' mission to the Guarini tribe in the mountains. On the trip there he carries a huge collection of metal shields, armor and pans. At one point a priest urges the priest-who has befriended De Niro, "Let him lay that burden down. Hasn't he carried it far enough?"

The priest replies, "He has chosen his own penance." The former slaver is trying to bend his perverse will back in the direction of the good, the true and the beautiful. These heavy tokens of his warrior past symbolize the burden of his guilt and remind him of what he has been redeemed from.

Sin bangs a nail into our soul. In reconciling us to the Father, Jesus removes the nail. The hole that remains, like that in a piece of wood, is the damage sin effects in our soul. It remains to be repaired if we are to be that radiant church, "without spot or wrinkle or any such thing," that she might be "holy and without blemish." This is the church that Jesus will take as his bride (see Ephesians 5:26–27).

Scripture offers us examples of those who found *eternal* forgiveness with God but whose sin led to tragic *temporal* consequences. Moses, for instance, expected to lead his people into the Promised Land. But he struck the rock twice in the wilderness instead of merely speaking to it as God had commanded. So God forbade his entrance into the Promised Land (see Numbers 20:1–12). Was Moses forgiven? We know he went to heaven because he appeared on the Mount of Transfiguration with Elijah (see Matthew 17:1–8; Luke 9:28–36). Though forgiven, Moses had to bear the temporal consequences of his sin.

Consider David and Bathsheba. The prophet Nathan confronted David for his treachery and adultery. David repented, but he and Bathsheba still suffered the loss of their firstborn son (see 2 Samuel 11:1—12:25).

The essence of Christianity is Christ's reproducing his life in us—his suffering, death and then his resurrection and glory. Penance is one of the ways God's love squeezes us into conformity to Christ. He loves us the way we are, but he loves us too much to let us stay that way. He accepts us where we are in order that he might move us to where he is. Our salvation and ultimate union with God is closely bound up with our willingness to suffer with Christ. Prayer, almsgiving and fasting have been common penances throughout salvation history (see Nehemiah 9:1–2).

> The Spirit himself [bears] witness with our spirit that we are children of God, and if children, then heirs, heirs of God and fellow heirs with Christ, provided we suffer with him in order that we may also be glorified with him. (Romans 8:16–17)

> Since therefore Christ suffered in the flesh, arm yourselves with the same thought, for whoever has suffered in the flesh has ceased from sin. (1 Peter 4:1)

> Love covers a multitude of sins. (1 Peter 4:8)

> In your struggle against sin you have not yet resisted to the point of shedding your blood. And have you forgotten the exhortation which addresses you as sons?—
> > My son, do not regard lightly the discipline of the Lord,
> > nor lose courage when you are punished by him.
> > For the Lord disciplines him whom he loves,
> > and chastises every son whom he receives.'
> > It is for discipline that you have to endure. God is treating you
> > as sons. (Hebrews 12:4–7)

> Our God is a consuming fire. (Hebrews 12:29; see also 1 Corinthians 3:10; Malachi 3:3; 4:1)

Throughout Scripture we find not only a forgiving God but a transforming, purifying and disciplining God. Discipline and forgiveness are not incompatible. Penance is a means by which God insures that we will not become habituated to patterns of life that will separate us from him. It is an amazing grace.

*D*on't Catholics just confess to a priest and then go out and do the same things again?

Yes, I often do. But I'm less inclined to repeat my sins knowing that I will shortly return to face Christ in the person of my priest-confessor.[1]

For Catholics there is truly only one Priest, Christ himself. Through ordination Father Bill's and Father Staley's souls receive a special imprint or configuration that makes them a carrier of the one priesthood of Jesus. Hearing confessions, then, is no functional chore for a priest; it is a sharing in the passion of Christ.

Saint Padre Pio, known for his apostolate of the confessional, exhorted his fellow priests: "Souls are not given as a gift: they are bought. Don't you know what they cost Jesus? They must be paid for with the same coin."[2]

In confession I have a much greater incentive to avoid repeating my sin than when I could quickly toss out the plea, "Forgive me," to the God in my thoughts. In both cases I earnestly and diligently confessed my sins. But now, as a Catholic, I do so in a concrete, interpersonal setting. I speak to an embodied man who stands "in the person of Christ" (see John 20:21; James 5:14–16).

This encounter urges a greater honesty, transparency and accountability as I confront the shame and guilt of my sin. Speaking one's sins to another—hearing it leave one's lips and knowing it enters the priest's ears—lends a gravity and objectivity to confession that are usually lacking when we confess to merely ourselves and our image of God at that moment. Light is thrown on our transgression from a source independent of ourselves.

Some find this prospect intimidating, but as Saint Jerome has written, "if the sick person is too ashamed to show his wound to the doctor, the medicine cannot heal what it does not know."[3] Christ's healing words of forgiveness may be thought, but they aren't heard when we avoid the sacrament of penance.

There is another value in confessing to another person with-you in space and time. That person can directly correct any hypercriticism or scrupulosity in your self-perception.

There's a funny story about a young woman entering the confessional and confessing that she suffered from the beset-ting sin of pride. "Father, it has taken such control over me that every time I'm at Mass and look around at other women, it dawns on me that I am the prettiest one in the entire assem-bly. What can I do to control this pride?"

The priest paused and said, "My child, that's not a sin. Why, that's just a mistake!"

While confession is not psychological counseling or therapy or even, strictly speaking, spiritual direction, it is an opportu-nity to get a reality check.[4] We hear the voice of Christ and not just our own inclinations. This is why Jesus entrusted the for-giving *and* retaining of sins to human agents (see John 20:21–23).

The sacrament of reconciliation offers a spiritual resurrec-tion and a radical reorientation of our whole life. We turn from evil and return to God.

> It makes sacramentally present Jesus' call to conversion, the first step in returning to the Father from whom one has strayed by sin [see Mark 1:15; Luke 15:18].... In this sacrament, the sinner, plac-ing himself before the merciful judgment of God, *anticipates* in a certain way the *judgment* to which he will be subjected at the end of his earthly life. For it is now, in this life, that we are offered the

choice between life and death, and it is only by the road of conversion that we can enter the Kingdom, from which one is excluded by grave sin. (*CCC,* #1423, 1470; see also 1 Corinthians 5:11; Galatians 5:19–21; Revelation 22:15)

What are some practical activities that bring forth these fruits befitting repentance?

Conversion is accomplished in daily life by gestures of reconciliation, concern for the poor, the exercise and defense of justice and right, by the admission of faults to one's brethren, fraternal correction, revision of life, examination of conscience, spiritual direction, acceptance of suffering, endurance of persecution for the sake of righteousness. Taking up one's cross each day and following Jesus is the surest way of penance. (*CCC,* #1435; see Amos 5:24; Isaiah 1:17; Luke 9:23)

What constitutes a good confession?

At least three elements: confession, contrition and penance.[5]

The Greek word for *confession, (homologeo)* simply means "to say the same thing as." When we confess our sins, we seek to have the same estimate of our transgressions as God does. We calmly examine our conscience in light of the Word of God. We measure our lives against the Ten Commandments, the Sermon on the Mount and the moral instructions of the apostolic letters.[6] Whatever we have done or failed to do, with full knowledge and consent, against the will of God, we confess to Christ in number and kind.

Contrition means a genuine sorrow for sin and the resolution not to sin again. We turn away from sin to God. Like the Prodigal Son, we have come to our senses and are returning broken to the Father, willing to do whatever is necessary to right the disordered condition we have created.

Genuine repentance is far more than a mere acknowledgment of the sin. It is all too common for a person to briefly express sorrow over a sin and then to reassure himself quickly with a verse of forgiveness like "He is faithful and just, and will forgive our sins" (1 John 1:9) and then move on. But this can produce a tremendous hardness of heart, especially in people who are falling repeatedly into a particular sin. We need to feel such grief over our offense that sin will appear as odious to us as it appears to God, and we are moved to fight fiercely against the wicked thing.

Contrition also means firmly purposing not to sin again. Given our weakness, we can't promise honestly that we will never fall into sin again. Even the most mature among us must guard against falling (see Galatians 6:1). We do, however, firmly purpose to avoid the occasions of sin, those settings and activities in which opportunities for sin are most common. The birds of temptation will continue flying through our head, but we will do our best to shoo them before they build a nest there, and we certainly aren't going to secure a place in our imagination for them to gather.

Then comes the test of our sorrow and resolve: Are we willing to make restitution for the damage we have created?

Penance seeks to undo the damage our sin has caused to our neighbors and to ourselves and to our relationship with God. Forgiveness takes away the guilt of sin, but it does not remedy all the disorders sin has caused. So we return stolen goods, restore the reputation of someone we slandered, fast to compensate for gluttony and so on.

When the priest establishes a penance, he takes into account the penitent's personal circumstances, the seriousness of the sin and what will best lead to the spiritual good of the sinner. Penances may consist of some simple prayer, almsgiving, fasting, works of mercy, self-denial, sacrifices and above all the patient acceptance of the cross we must bear.

> Jesus' call to conversion and penance, like that of the prophets before him, does not aim first at outward works, 'sackcloth and ashes,' fasting and mortification, but at the conversion of the heart, interior conversion [see 2 Corinthians 4:16; Ephesians 3:16]. Without this, such penances remain sterile and false; however, interior conversion urges expression in visible signs, gestures and works of penance. (*CCC,* #1430; see also #1459–1460; Revelation 2:5, 16)

In the sacrament of reconciliation we are restored to fellowship with God and his family. Christ tangibly reaches out to us and touches us in the person of the priest. The words of absolution are the very words of God. To most, even good people, God is a belief. To the saints God is an embrace. We will never feel as hugged by our heavenly Father as when we confess our sins and hear God's absolving us of them.

Pope John Paul II urged us: "To those who have been far away from the sacrament of Reconciliation and forgiving love, I make this appeal: Come back to this source of grace; do not be afraid! Christ himself is waiting for you. He will heal you, and you will be at peace with God!"[7]

Why do Catholics celebrate the Eucharist every Sunday?

Saint Paul wrote, "As often as you eat this bread and drink the cup, you proclaim the Lord's death until he comes" (1 Corinthians 11:26). Since the celebration of the Eucharist is a proclamation of the gospel, the Catholic church offers the liturgy every day throughout the year, with the exception of Good Friday.

The earliest Christians shared a love feast in which they also shared the Eucharist. It was a daily affair: "They devoted themselves to the apostles' teaching and fellowship, to the breaking of bread and the prayers.... Day by day, attending the temple together and breaking bread in their homes, they partook of food with glad and generous hearts" (Acts 2:42, 46; see 1 Corinthians 11:20–34). They recalled the children of Israel in the wilderness, who daily received the heavenly manna (see Exodus 16). Daily communion with the Lord through the breaking of bread also seemed to fulfill their plea, "Give us this day our daily bread" (Matthew 6:11).

The chief communal celebration of Christ's dying and rising, however, remained the "first day of the week," as it still is today (see Acts 20:7; 1 Corinthians 16:2). Each Sunday was a little Easter, the day of resurrection. The *Didache* describes the breaking of bread as occurring on "the Lord's Day" (*Didache*, 14:1). Pagan observers, like Pliny, noted that Christians came together on "a fixed day."[8] The Christian apologist Justin Martyr described Christians receiving the Lord's Supper on a day called Sunday.[9]

The early church was eucharistic: without the Eucharist there was no church. Before there was a sacramental theology of the Eucharist, there was the liturgy of the Eucharist.[10] Cyprian, Jerome, John Chrysostom and Ambrose all mention the continued daily reception of the Eucharist. Chrysostom even claimed that Christians were to receive Communion as often as the Eucharist was celebrated. Augustine summarized the state of things in the late fourth and early fifth century: "Some partake daily of the body and blood of Christ, others receive it on stated days: in some places no day passes without the sacrifice being offered; in others it is only on Saturday and the Lord's day, or it may be only on the Lord's day."[11]

While some Christian communities restrict Communion to once a month or even once a year, the Catholic church, as well as Lutherans, Episcopalians and the Eastern Orthodox, believe this ignores the practice of the apostolic church and unwittingly undermines the purpose of the sacrament, which is to convey grace and publicly bear witness to the Lord's death and coming again.

Lay reception of Communion waxed and waned throughout the Middle Ages, and strangely, in this so-called age of faith, reception of the Eucharist was probably less common than at any other period in church history. The teaching of the great theologians, like Peter Lombard and Thomas Aquinas, however, favored frequent, even daily Communion. Various reformers like Catherine of Siena, Vincent Ferrer and Ignatius Loyola urged a return to frequent reception.

The fruits of frequent Communion are sweet. Holy Communion augments our union with Christ, separates us from sin, strengthens the bond of charity toward others, commits us to the poor, increases our hunger for visible unity with other Christians and is a pledge of glory to come (see *CCC*, #1391–1405).

> [Today] the Church obliges the faithful to take part in the Divine Liturgy on Sundays and feast days and, prepared by the sacrament of Reconciliation, to receive the Eucharist at least once a year, if possible during the Easter season. But the Church strongly encourages the faithful to receive the holy Eucharist on Sundays and feast days, or more often still, even daily.... Thus from celebration to celebration, as they proclaim the Paschal mystery of Jesus "until he comes," the pilgrim People of God advances, "following the narrow way of the cross," toward the heavenly banquet, when all the elect will be seated at the table of the kingdom. (*CCC*, #1389, 1344)

Is it true that Catholics believe Christ is sacrificed again at every Mass?

The Mass is not a re-sacrifice of Christ; it is the one sacrifice of Christ on Calvary re-presented. "He has appeared *once for all* at the end of the age to put away sin by the sacrifice of himself.... *Once for all*...he offered up himself.... We have been sanctified through the offering of the body of Jesus Christ *once for all*" (Hebrews 9:26; 7:27; 10:10; emphasis added; see *CCC*, #571).

So it is fairly asked, "How is the 'once-for-all' historical sacrifice of Christ on Calvary made contemporaneous, present with us today? How can I be present at an event that happened once in history?" The fathers answer the question in two related but distinct ways.

First, they stress the "trans-temporal" quality of the Eucharist. The Eucharist not only looks back to the crucifixion but looks forward to the Second Coming. "For as often as you eat this bread and drink the cup, you proclaim the Lord's death until he comes" (1 Corinthians 11:26). The Lord's Supper is celebrated on the first day of the new creation, i.e. the "eighth day," Sunday, the little Easter, the events which gave rise to it inaugurated the age to come. Thus it is called the sacrifice of the last days.[12] So the Eucharist occurs in the present, and it looks to the past (the crucifixion) and to the future (the Day of the Lord, the Second Coming).

The Jewish Passover also has this "trans-temporal" quality. In the *Haggadah* of the Passover seder, the Jews also look to the past and future simultaneously. In the first question of the seder, the youngest child in the family asks: "Why *is this night* different from all other nights?" Then the father recites the biblical account of the deliverance from Egypt. So the Passover seder looks backward (see Deuteronomy 6:20–25; Exodus 12; 13:17–15:5).

Later the covenantal promise is invoked for the present and future: "And this [promise] is what has stood by our ancestors and by us, that not only one time have they [enemies of Israel] opposed us and tried to destroy us, but in each and every generation they oppose us and try to destroy us, but The Holy One, Blessed Be He, has saved us from their hands" (see Genesis 15:7). At the end of the seder it is always said, "Next year in Jerusalem!" which makes the sacred, ancient moment of liberation a sign of hope. By this ritual action Jews of every generation participate in God's historic act of deliverance.[13]

Saint Paul tightens the link between the deliverance of the children of Israel from Egypt and the salvation Christ offers to his followers in the Eucharist:

> I want you to know, brethren, that our fathers were all under the cloud, and all passed through the sea, and all were baptized into Moses in the cloud and in the sea, and all ate the same supernatural food and all drank the same supernatural drink. For they drank from the supernatural Rock which followed them, and the Rock was Christ.... The cup of blessing which we bless, is it not a participation in the blood of Christ? The bread which we break, is it not a participation in the body of Christ? (1 Corinthians 10:1–4, 16)

In the Mass we look back to our redemption achieved and forward to our redemption fulfilled. Almost all the eucharistic prayers in the Roman Missal look forward to the coming of the Lord in glory. This is especially so during Advent, as we wait for Christ's coming. The memorial acclamation anticipates Jesus' return: "Christ has died, Christ is risen, Christ will come again." Just before Holy Communion we hear the phrase, "Happy are those who are called to his supper," inviting us to the wedding supper of the Lamb in the fully realized kingdom (see Matthew 26:29; Luke 22:29–30; Revelation 3:20; 19:9). Even in the present, the church already sits at table with Christ to eat and drink with him (see *CCC,* #1000, 1326, 1402–1405, 1419).

While the church fathers taught the "trans-temporal" aspect of the Eucharist, they also emphasized its "supra-temporal" aspect. That is, it originates outside of time. From the standpoint of time, the Lord Jesus sacrificed his life once for all time outside of Jerusalem on Golgotha. From the standpoint of eternity, however, his offering stands outside of time, since he is "a lamb without blemish or spot.... He was destined *before* the foundation of the world" (1 Peter 1:19–20; emphasis added).

The earthly liturgy is but the counterpart of the heavenly, and it is from heaven that it receives its saving power. In the celebration of the Eucharist, we gather with the entire company of heaven in the sacred place where time intersects eternity. The eternal sacrifice is perpetually carried out in the Son's obedience to the Father from all eternity. The Trinity as well as Calvary is made visible during the Mass, the paschal mystery.

This is far more than a memorial service on behalf of one who has passed on. We find the crucified and risen Christ in our midst: "This *is* my body, this *is* my blood.... This *is* the Lamb of God who takes away the sin of the world." The Eastern Orthodox share this understanding:

> During the Liturgy, through its divine power, we are projected to the point where eternity cuts across time, and at this point we become true contemporaries with the events which we commemorate.... All the holy suppers of the Church are nothing else than one eternal and unique Supper, that of Christ in the Upper Room. The same divine act both takes place at a specific moment in history, and is offered always in the sacrament.[14]

So in answer to the question, "How can I be present at an

event that happened once in history?" Catholics answer: "The event (Calvary) and the ritual activity presenting the event (Eucharist) look backward and forward at the same time. Further, the event originates in eternity, outside of time, and is thereby accessible at every moment of time."[15]

So the Mass is not a repetition of Christ's sacrifice but a re-presentation of it, beckoning us to presently enter into it through sacred space and time. God is not only everywhere; he is every-when. He occupies not only every place but every moment.

Thus, in the Eucharist we become true contemporaries with the great saving event of the new covenant. We are there on Golgotha in communion with the sacrifice "...before the foundation of the world...of the Lamb that was slain" (Revelation 13:8). Thus Christ does not die each time a Mass is offered. Rather the nearly three hundred thousand "Holy Sacrifices of the Mass" performed each day are nothing but the one, eternal and unique sacrificial meal Christ instituted in the Upper Room with his apostles applied to particular moments of space and time. The same Jesus who died and rose again is now with us. The whole congregation unites itself with his holy sacrificial will and consecrates itself to the heavenly Father as a living sacrifice.

This is why Catholics celebrate the Holy "Sacrifice" of the Mass. Further, the sacrifice of Christ and the sacrifice of the Eucharist are one single sacrifice in which *we*, united with him, *offer ourselves to God.* Saint Augustine writes: "This is the sacrifice of Christians: we, being many, are one body in Christ. And this also is the sacrifice which the Church continually celebrates in the sacrament of the altar, known to the faithful, in which she teaches that she herself is offered in the offering she makes to God."[16]

Some have tried to deny that the early church understood the Eucharist as a sacrifice (see *CCC,* #1362–1372). The surest interpreters, however, are those nearest the writing of the New Testament. For example, Clement of Rome (fl. c. 97), whom Irenaeus of Lyons (c. 130–c. 200) claims knew Peter and Paul,[17] wrote around A.D. 96 of bishops "who blamelessly and holily have offered its sacrifices." He draws parallels between the church's ministers and the Old Testament priests and Levites.[18] Ignatius of Antioch writes of "one altar for the whole Church, and one bishop" and so connects Eucharist and sacrifice.[19] The *Didache,* or *The Teaching of the Twelve,* is the oldest surviving church order, and predictably, it describes early eucharistic practice:

> Assemble on the Lord's day, and break bread and offer the Eucharist; but first make confession of your faults, so that your *sacrifice* may be a pure one. Anyone who has a difference with his fellow is not to take part with you until he has been reconciled, so as to avoid any profanation of your sacrifice [Matthew 5:23–24]. For this is the *offering* of which the Lord has said, "Everywhere and always bring me a *sacrifice* that is undefiled, for I am a great king, says the Lord, and my name is the wonder of nations" [Malachi 1:11, 14].[20]

For Irenaeus the Eucharist is "the new oblation of the new covenant."[21] Later Cyril, bishop of Jerusalem (c. 315–386), can say that "we offer…Christ sacrificed for our sins."[22]

By the end of the fourth century there is a strong sense in some writers that the worshipper at the Eucharist stands in the presence of Christ sacrificed. Saint John Chrysostom (347–407), for example, speaks of "the most dread sacrifice" offered by the priest in the company of the angels and all the powers of heaven, "in honor of Him who lieth" on the altar."[23]

Historian of doctrine J.N.D. Kelly observes that "it was natural for early Christians to think of the eucharist as a sacrifice.

The fulfillment of prophecy demanded a solemn Christian offering, and the rite itself was wrapped in the sacrificial atmosphere with which our Lord invested the Last Supper."[24]

Yes, the Mass is a sacrifice, but it is not the cross redone; it is the cross applied, continued and perpetuated. This Eucharist is "the source and summit of the Christian life" because it is the sacrificial life of Christ (*Lumen gentium,* 11).[25]

Why do Catholics call Mary Coredemptrix?

Let's be clear. Jesus is the redeemer of humanity; Mary is not. Further, while "Mary, Coredemptrix" has been part of Catholic thought and devotion, it is not yet clear whether this title will receive dogmatic definition. In 1997 *Newsweek* carried a cover story on the possibility of just such a definition.[26]

All admit, however, that this designation of Mary has long been part of the devotional life of the church and further developed during the pontificates of Popes Pius X, Pius XI and John Paul II. Blessed Mother Teresa of Calcutta, though no systematic theologian, wrote: "The papal definition of Mary as Coredemptrix, Mediatrix and Advocate will bring great graces to the Church."[27]

As did Mother Teresa, the church usually considers Coredemptrix in connection with two other titles: Mediatrix and Advocate. These three are understood together under the rubric of Mary's maternal mediation.

> Mary, having been providentially prepared by the Father through her Immaculate Conception, uniquely participated with Jesus Christ, the divine Saviour of humanity as Coredemptrix with the Redeemer, by her free and active fiat the Annunciation and her faithful perseverance in union with her Son unto the Cross. After her Assumption into heaven, Mary continues this saving office in

> service to Christ the one Mediator as Mediatrix of all grace and gifts
> of eternal salvation, which she performs in intimate union with the
> Holy Spirit, the Sanctifier. Mary further continues to intercede on
> behalf of the human family before the throne of Christ, victorious
> King of all nations, as Advocate for the People of God. Thus the
> maternal and universal mediation of the Mother of Jesus are man-
> ifested in these three essential doctrinal roles: Coredemptrix,
> Mediatrix, Advocate.[28]

The first application of the word *Coredemptrix* to Mary appears
to date back to the fourteenth century, to a liturgical book
found in St. Peter's Church in Salzburg.[29] The concept, however, is already present in the writings of Irenaeus and Justin
Martyr in the idea of the Second Eve.

Just as Adam and Eve killed the life of God dwelling within
them by disobedience, so too do the Last Adam and the New
Eve restore that life by obedience to the will of God. Eve hands
the instrument of death to Adam in the Garden; Mary hands
Jesus the instrument, a body, that brings eternal life (see
Hebrews 10:10). Pope Pius XII stated that "it was she, the
second Eve, who...offered Him on Golgotha to the Eternal
Father for all the children of Adam, sin-stained by his unhappy
fall, and her mother's rights and mother's love were included
in the holocaust."[30]

Unfortunately, in English *coredemptrix* sounds like *cochair*
or *cocaptain*, implying that Jesus needed to split the office of
Redeemer with someone else because the task of dying for the
sins of the world was just a little too much for him. Rather, the
co in *coredemptrix* refers to a "cooperator" or "collaborator"
with the Redeemer.

The Word of God never places Mary on a level of equality
with Jesus Christ. Mary is everything that she is through Christ.
She needed a Savior, and her Savior was Jesus Christ. But her
divine maternity is an unparalleled sharing in the mysterious

work of the divine Redeemer. To say that she plays a singular role in salvation history is not to claim that she is equal to the Redeemer.

Redemption is first prophesied immediately after the original sin. God rebukes the serpent: "I will put enmity between you and the woman, / and between your seed and her seed; / he shall bruise your head, / and you shall bruise his heel" (Genesis 3:15). In this "proto-evangelium" or "first gospel," we hear the ground bass motif that will recur throughout salvation's song: "the Woman" is "with the Redeemer."

This pattern is heard repeatedly in Scripture: "Behold, a young woman shall conceive and bear a son, and shall call his name Emmanuel" (Isaiah 7:14; Matthew 1:23). So too, "when the time had fully come, God sent forth his Son, born of woman" (Galatians 4:4). At the Annunciation, when the angel Gabriel hailed her as "full of grace," Mary said "yes" to God's plan and donated her flesh to the Word made flesh (see John 1:14). She cooperated with the Savior in a way beyond that of any other creature in heaven or on earth.

But her "yes" at the Annunciation and her motherhood at the Nativity only begin her union with her Son in his work of salvation (see *Lumen gentium,* 57). Simeon, inspired by the Spirit, attends the presentation of Jesus in the temple. Cradling the infant, he exclaims, "Lord, now lettest thou thy servant depart in peace, / according to thy word; / for mine eyes have seen thy salvation / which thou hast prepared in the presence of all peoples" (Luke 2:29–31). But then he turns to the Mother of the Redeemer: "Behold, this child is set for the fall and rising of many in Israel, / and for a sign that is spoken against (and a sword will pierce through your soul also)" (Luke 2:34–35). Jesus' mission of redemptive suffering will cause profound suffering for her as well. The Woman will suffer with the Savior.

Simeon's words lead Mary to the foot of the cross.

> Standing by the cross of Jesus were his mother.... When Jesus saw his mother, and the disciple whom he loved standing near, he said to his mother, "Woman, behold, your son!" Then he said to the disciple, "Behold, your mother!" And from that hour the disciple took her to his own home. After this Jesus, knowing that all was now finished...said, "It is finished"; and he bowed his head and gave up his spirit. (John 19:25–28, 30)

Here the "woman" who is the mother of the Savior is linked with the "woman" whose seed will crush the head of the serpent and destroy sin and death.

> Thus the Blessed Virgin advanced in her pilgrimage of faith, and faithfully persevered in her union with her Son unto the cross, where she stood, in keeping with the divine command, enduring with her only begotten Son the intensity of his suffering, associated herself with his sacrifice in her mother's heart, and lovingly consenting to the immolation of this victim which was born of her. (*Lumen gentium,* 58; see 62)

While no one can do the work that Jesus did in securing redemption, Saint Paul teaches that we can join our suffering to his and that such suffering is fruitful for the salvation of others: "Now I rejoice in my sufferings for your sake, and in my flesh I complete what is lacking in Christ's afflictions for the sake of his body, that is, the church" (Colossians 1:24; see also Philippians 3:10–11). Paul is certainly not disparaging the work of Jesus as being inadequate or needing a little more oomph. Rather the living Christ is acting through Paul's sufferings, and Paul's sufferings are extending Christ's redemptive work.

So too John Paul II wrote of Mary's "spiritual crucifixion" at the foot of the cross: "As a witness to her Son's passion by her presence, and as a sharer in it by her compassion, Mary offered a unique contribution to the Gospel of suffering, by embodying in anticipation, the expression of St. Paul.... She truly has a special title to be able to claim that she 'completes in her flesh'—as already in her heart—'what is lacking in the suffering of Christ.'"[31] In an address in Ecuador he stated: "Crucified spiritually with her crucified Son (cf. Gal 2:20), she contemplated with heroic love the death of her God."[32]

This is what is meant by the title "Coredemptrix": not a claim to equality with Christ but an obedient and free cooperation with him in suffering for the sake of the gospel. Those of us who preach the gospel or perform other apostolic work become "God's fellow workers" (1 Corinthians 3:9; see also 2 Corinthians 6:1; 1 Thessalonians 3:2).

While a hot brick warms, it receives its warmth from something other than itself, some heat source like a furnace. While the furnace is the "Warmer," the brick warmed by the furnace mediates the furnace's heat to others. In this sense the brick can be called a "co-warmer."

Mary receives the title "Coredemptrix" because of her unique maternity. She holds the title for all of us since she is the Mother of all Christians. Under her feet the God of peace will crush Satan (see Romans 16:20).[33]

Part III
Worship and Devotion

What is the liturgical year?

The liturgical year (the church calendar) is the Catholic church's antidote to spiritual attention deficit hyperactivity disorder. By commemorating Easter (the Resurrection of Jesus), the conversion of Saint Paul (January 25), the martyrs under the Roman Emperor Nero (June 30), the beheading of John the Baptist (August 29), Saint Francis of Assisi (October 4), Saint Joseph (March 19) and scores of other dates, we daily and annually settle our jumpy minds and fix our wandering hearts on the great events and agents of salvation history and say "no" to the onslaught of consumeristic, competitive, impersonal mass culture.

But the liturgical calendar is more than just a way of commandeering our attention; it cures our spiritual amnesia so we can give honor where honor is due. Because we have a tendency to forget God's divine favors ("They forgot what he had done, and the miracles that he had shown them"), the liturgical year systematically brings to our remembrance "the wonderful works that he has done" (Psalm 78:1; 1 Chronicles 16:12).[1] Then we can shower upon the great personalities and events of redemption the reverence they deserve. Vatican II explained: "In the course of the year…[the church] unfolds the whole mystery of Christ from the incarnation and nativity to the ascension to Pentecost and the expectation of the blessed hope of the coming of the Lord" (*Sacrosanctum Concilium,* 102).[2]

For many the connection between calendars and spirituality is not immediately evident. But time is the sphere of creation in which God's plan is actualized. God is not only the plan's author but a player in the drama of carrying it out. He calls Abraham. He leads Israel in the Exodus. He is a warrior in the conquest of the Promised Land. He is victim and victor in the crucifixion and Resurrection. He gives the Holy Spirit on the Feast of Pentecost. With Christ the kingdom of God has penetrated the kingdom of this world, and "all our created time…has become 'porous' to God."[3]

God impregnates history, and at any instant he might midwife us into eternity; any moment may reveal the decisive unveiling of the everlasting. Our attention catches a naked glimpse of eternity, yet the veil falls too quickly back over our eyes. Time passes, our memory fades, our willpower weakens, our restless attention flitters between the urgent and the important, the trivial and the profound. This is where the liturgical calendar arrests our attention and arranges the great mysteries of redemption in a cyclical order resplendent in coordinated colors, vestments, music, Scripture readings, liturgical texts, group petitions and spiritual disciplines of fasting, feasting, abstinences, prayer, intercessions, meditations, penances and pilgrimages.

It's a happy, blessed assault on our senses, heart and mind. In and of itself, time saves nothing and improves nothing. Through the church calendar Christ structures time to assist in our sanctification. Make "the most of the time," urges Saint Paul, "because the days are evil" (Ephesians 5:16; see also Colossians 4:5). Observing the liturgical calendar turns evil to good.

Some complain, "What's all this fuss about marking time? Aren't all days the same? Can't I worship God on Tuesday as well as on Sunday?" They cite Saint Paul: "Let no one pass judgment on you in questions of food and drink or with regard to a festival or a new moon or a sabbath. These are only a shadow of what is to come; but the substance belongs to Christ" (Colossians 2:16; see also Romans 14:5; Galatians 4:10).

Every day is the day that the Lord has made, and all days are to be lived as sacred (see Psalm 118:24).

Well, yes and no. God likes days and hours and seasons; they were his ideas. And Paul's objection was not to a liturgical calendar. The festivals to which he objected were intended to heighten awareness of the coming messiah. This seemed foolish to Paul, since these festivals implicitly denied that the Messiah had come, as they did not celebrate Jesus as Lord. But communal observance of days of worship has always been part of being the people of God.

In the Ten Commandments God told the children of Israel to "remember the sabbath day, to keep it holy. Six days you shall labor, and do all your work; but the seventh day is a sabbath to the LORD your God" (Exodus 20:8–10; Deuteronomy 5:12–14). Sometimes by his direct command, sometimes by wise custom, the Hebrews observed feasts and fixed festivals like Passover, Rosh Hashanah, Pentecost, Yom Kippur and others.[4] In this way they honored God's mighty deeds in history, gave thanks to him for his goodness toward them, insured the perpetual remembrance of these deeds and instructed the next generation so that they might know and love this God who acts in space and time (see *CCC*, #1164).

This principle of communal sacred observances continues in the New Testament and the church. In the Gospels we observe Jesus teaching in the synagogue on the Sabbath (see Luke 4:16). Christ is raised on the day after the Sabbath, "the first day of the week" (see Matthew 28:1; Mark 16:2; Luke 24:1; John 20:1, 19).

One week later to the day, the apostles gather together, and this weekly reunion becomes "the Lord's day."[5] Some have even called Sunday the "lord of days." Corporate worship on this first day of the week receives several mentions in the New

Testament: "On the first day of the week, when we were gathered together to break bread" (Acts 20:7; see 1 Corinthians 16:2; Revelation 1:10; *Didache,* 14:1).

Perhaps the oldest evidence of a primitive church year—that is, an annual remembrance—is found in Paul's First Letter to the Corinthians of A.D. 57. Here Paul refers to "Christ, our paschal lamb" and urges Christians to "celebrate the festival" (1 Corinthians 5:7–8). This reference seems to suggest that the early Christians celebrated the death and resurrection of Christ during the Jewish Passover. We know that by the end of the second century, at least, the Roman church had an annual resurrection celebration on a spring Sunday as well as the weekly observance of Sunday, the day of the Lord's resurrection.

Easter and Pentecost were both observed from the first as Jewish festivals with a new Christian significance. The Acts of the Apostles recounts the outpouring of the Holy Spirit on the day of the Old Testament feast of Pentecost (Greek for *fiftieth*). It was natural for the church to reverence this event fifty days after the annual Easter festival (see Acts 2:1).

Easter was also the annual time to baptize new members. By the seventh century a forty-day period of penitence and instruction preceded the Easter baptisms. These forty days imitated Jesus' forty-day period of fasting and trial in the desert and came to be called "Lent."

Another cycle of seasonal feasts grew up around the celebration of Christ's incarnation, including Advent, Christmas and Epiphany. Various methods have been used to calculate the date of Christ's actual Nativity. January 2, April 18, April 29, May 20 as well as December 25 were suggested. The church chose December 25 because it coincided with the pagan festivals of Saturnalia and the winter solstice. The church thus combated paganism by displacing rather than abolishing their festivals and offered the pagan world the true fulfillment of their transcendent aspirations. The "sun of righteousness" in Malachi 4:2 replaced the sun god, Sol Invictus, whose pagan feast was celebrated on December 25.

There also developed memorials to the saints. "By celebrating their anniversaries the Church proclaims achievement of the paschal mystery in the saints who have suffered and have been glorified with Christ" (*Sacrosanctum Concilium*, 103–104).

Lastly, Christians began regularly fasting on Wednesdays and Fridays.[6]

While the Jews had a number of divinely commanded sabbaths and seven set feasts, the Christian liturgical year evolved over centuries. A few representative alterations include Pius V's sixteenth-century schema dealing with Mary and the saints. In 1955 Pius XII established the Feast of Saint Joseph the Worker to offer a Christian view of work in response to communist May Day celebrations. Pope Paul VI, in February 1969, published norms for a revised calendar for the Western church in *Mysterii Paschalis*. In a decree dated May 23, 2000, the Congregation for Divine Worship named the Second Sunday of Easter "Divine Mercy" Sunday, to help the "Christian world to face, with confidence in divine benevolence, the difficulties and trials that mankind will experience in the years to come."[7]

Revision is an ongoing work. "The liturgical year is to be revised so that the traditional customs and discipline of the sacred seasons shall be preserved or restored to suit the conditions of modern times" (*Sacrosanctum Concilium*, 107). The French Benedictine monk Prosper Louis Gueranger (1805–1875) is often called the Father of the Modern Liturgical Movement. Among his many liturgical works is *L'année*

Liturgique (1841–1866), a comprehensive and devotional study of the church calendar.

Even though the liturgical year can be revised, its principle endures: Together, God's people must remember God's mighty works.

Not only did God reveal the principle of communal sacred observance, but the setting aside of days is inevitable. We are meaning-seeking creatures and will tease significance out of time. For instance, every Christian community recognizes the value of gathering on the day of the Lord's resurrection. That is supplemented by some Easter and Christmas observance at minimum. But "[m]ore than two events occurred in the gospel drama," says the ancient Church. There is a whole sequence of mysterious and marvelous events that the Lord passed through in His life here on earth, each one of which is most glorious in its significance and most salutary for us to think on."[8]

In a look at over forty United States denominations and fellowships, including those unsympathetic to liturgical calendars, it becomes clear that, to a more or less degree, each has a calendar.[9] There is no avoiding organizing our lives and corporate worship according to times and seasons. The question is who or what will shape and order the church's gatherings. Will it be the secular, civil society? Will it be denominational concerns? Will it be the mighty acts of God and the men and women whose lives are towering models of holiness?

The Assemblies of God, for instance, is a Pentecostal denomination and part of the free-church tradition, meaning each local church is "free" to establish its own worship calendar as well as many other matters. It is known for prizing spontaneous praise and asking the Holy Spirit to guide its worship. The denomination does, however, publish a "Pastor's Planbook" and a "Master Calendar."

For the Assemblies the new year begins just like the civil calendar, on January 1. The only Christian events printed on the calendar are Palm Sunday, Good Friday, Easter, Pentecost Sunday, Reformation Day and Christmas. Listings for denominational programs comprise the greatest number of events. For instance, Teen Challenge, Royal Rangers, women's ministries, military personnel and many others all have their special day for preaching about and collecting money for their particular ministry. Ecumenical events like Sanctity of Human Life Sunday and the National Day of Prayer are listed along with American holidays, including Martin Luther King Day, Father's Day, Labor Day and Columbus Day. When the Christian, denominational, ecumenical, national and civil holidays are accounted for, only seventeen Sundays on the 1992 calendar are left entirely open.[10] Human beings, by our very nature, invest time with meaning.

We all know that simply assenting to a truth doesn't immediately conform our lives to that truth. It's a beginning, but we need to circle back repeatedly and reappropriate those truths if they are to transform us. Keeping the liturgical calendar is no guarantee of blessedness, but it is a powerful aid for those whose hearts are disposed to cooperate with God's grace. Through observance of the liturgical calendar we remember our redemption, enliven our memory and sanctify the present time. We not only commemorate the past but actually live again the realities we are celebrating. We enter the "today" of the redemptive event (see *CCC,* #1165; Matthew 6:11; Hebrews 3:7–4:11; Psalm 95:7). (The liturgical calendar is available online. See www.catholicculture.org/lit/overviews/lit_year_main.cfm.)

*W*hat are solemnities, feasts and memorials?

These are technical words that refer to days with differing degrees of significance to the church.

Solemnities celebrate events, beliefs and persons of great importance and universal significance in salvation history. They eclipse all other feasts and memorials. Easter and Christmas are the greatest solemnities, with Easter being the Sunday of Sundays. Their observance begins with Evening Prayer of the preceding day.

Of the seventeen solemnities, nine refer to events in salvation history (for example, the Immaculate Conception, Christmas, Epiphany, the Annunciation, Easter, the Ascension, Pentecost, the birth of John the Baptist, the Assumption of Mary). Four refer to key persons in salvation history (Mary, Mother of God; Joseph, her husband; the apostles Peter and Paul; and All Saints' Day). Four focus on particular qualities of God and Christ (the Trinity, the Sacred Heart, Christ the King, the Body and Blood of Christ).

Feasts are less significant than solemnities but are tied frequently to key biblical and historical events. Some examples include the Baptism of the Lord, the conversion of Saint Paul, the chair of Saint Peter, the Holy Innocents, the guardian angels, the birth of Mary, the Transfiguration of the Lord and Mary's visit to Elizabeth.

Memorials are least significant and are never observed during Holy Week, the octave of Easter or the week preceding Christmas. Most saints' days are memorials and come in two forms: obligatory and optional. Obligatory memorials are universally celebrated. Optional memorials are important to a local country, church or religious community.[11]

For the most part, memorials put on view admirable men and women proposed by the church for our emulation. These saints are proof positive of what God intended for human life and of Christ's resurrection power in achieving it. Commemorations of saints are normally observed on their day of death and entry into heavenly glory. Birthdays are not celebrated because one is born into original sin.

There are two exceptions to this general rule. We celebrate the birth of John the Baptist, who Scripture tells us was sanctified in his mother's womb (see Luke 1:15), on June 24. Mary was conceived without the taint of original sin. We celebrate this on the Feast of the Immaculate Conception, December 8, and her birth nine months later on September 8.

Some examples of saints and their memorials are:

- ❖ Francis of Assisi, October 4, deacon: patron saint of Italy, Catholic action, ecology and animals

- ❖ Matthew, September 21, evangelist: patron of bankers

- ❖ Nicholas of Myra, December 6, bishop: patron of children

- ❖ Augustine, August 28, bishop and doctor of the church: patron of theologians

- ❖ Joseph of Arimathea, March 17: patron of funeral directors

- ❖ Francis de Sales, January 24, bishop and doctor: patron of authors and journalists

- ❖ Cecilia, November 22, virgin martyr: patroness of musicians

❖ Thomas Aquinas, January 28, priest and doctor of the church: patron of schools

❖ Our Lady of the Rosary, October 7

❖ John, December 27, evangelist: patron of painters

❖ Mary Magdalene, July 22: patroness of penitents

All Sundays are holy days of obligation, as are several other solemnities that do not fall on Sunday. What sets holy days of obligation apart from other feasts and memorials is that they require Christians to "participate in Mass…[and] abstain from those labors and business concerns which impede the worship to be rendered to God, the joy which is proper to the Lord's Day, or the proper relaxation of mind and body" (canon 1247).

The ten holy days of obligation recognized by canon law are Christmas, Mary the Mother of God, Epiphany, Saint Joseph, Saints Peter and Paul, the Ascension, *Corpus Christi,* the Assumption, All Saints and the Immaculate Conception. All holy days of obligation are solemnities, but three solemnities are not holy days of obligation: the Birth of John the Baptist, the Feast of the Sacred Heart and the Feast of the Annunciation.

With the approval of the pope, conferences of bishops can transfer or remove certain holy days of obligation. Consequently, the number of days varies from nation to nation. In the United States Epiphany and *Corpus Christi* are trans-ferred to the nearest Sunday. The obligation on the feasts of Saints Peter and Paul and Saint Joseph has been removed.

What are the portions of the liturgical year?

The resurrection of Jesus is the center of the Christian calendar. Every Sunday is, first of all, a "little Easter," "the Lord's Day," "the foundation and kernel of the whole liturgical year" (*Sacrosanctum Concilium*, 102). The celebration of the Resurrection might be called "the central organizing principle" of the Christian year, the light by which the rest of the year is seen.

Even Christmas is a mere candle compared to the blazing sun of Easter.[12] After all, everybody is born, but Christ alone rose from the dead.

Another way of describing the centrality of the Resurrection is to call it the sun around which everything else orbits. Imagine concentric circles around a fixed core. As we progress outward from the center through the orbits, we encounter in the orbit closest to our radiating hub Sundays, followed by Easter, Lent, Christmas and Advent. In the next orbit we have Mary, and in the outermost orbit, the saints and martyrs.

In the course of the year, then, the church celebrates the Resurrection every Sunday. She also celebrates it once every year, as well as "the whole mystery of Christ from the incarnation and nativity to the ascension, to Pentecost and the expectation of the blessed hope of the coming of the Lord" (*Sacrosanctum Concilium,* 102).

Because Mary, the Mother of God, is inseparably linked with her Son, days honoring her naturally arise. She is already the faultless image that the church aspires to become.

The church also observes memorial days of the martyrs and other saints. Since Christ's suffering and resurrection have been fully manifest in them, they are held up for us as models. The

Christian year becomes the medium through which we reenter the mysteries of redemption and encounter those who are already perfected in Christlikeness.

The calendar is actually composed of two different calendars that run concurrently: the "temporal cycle" (the Proper of Time) and the "sanctoral cycle" (the Proper of the Saints).

The temporal cycle (Latin, *temporalis,* "relating to time") contains three seasons: Christmas season, Paschal season and Ordinary Time, with its moveable Feasts of the Trinity, the Body of Christ *(Corpus Christi),* the Sacred Heart, Divine Mercy and Christ the King. The temporal cycle deals chiefly with the "times" and "events" of redemption.

The sanctoral cycle (Latin, *sanctus,* "saintly, holy") runs through the entire year alongside the temporal.[13] From its title one might hazard that its chief focus is the saints. Which it is, along with the Blessed Virgin and the angels. Every day has its saint or saints. Further, these are fixed feasts and memorials, while the temporal cycle is largely movable, based as it is on the date of Easter.

Easter Sunday is the first Sunday after the first full moon following the vernal equinox. It comes between March 22 and April 25. Ash Wednesday, the beginning of Lent, is calculated backward from Easter Sunday; Pentecost, by projecting forward. Christmas Day is the most significant immoveable solemnity. Again, the first Sunday in Advent is determined by calculating backward from December 25; the Baptism of Our Lord by counting forward.

Moveable feasts are always on the same day of the week; hence Ash Wednesday, Palm Sunday, Good Friday, Ascension Thursday. Bishops' conferences have the authority to move some feasts to the nearest Sunday.

The immoveable feasts are always on the same date of the month. The Feast of the Annunciation, for instance, is always March 25, exactly nine months (the common length of a pregnancy) before the birth of Jesus. The only exception is when March 25 falls within Holy Week or Easter Week; then the feast is celebrated the Monday after the octave of Easter.

Here's an important point: the temporal cycle presents the mysteries of Christ's redemption, so it always takes priority over the sanctoral cycle, which presents those persons who are the fruit of that redemption. The temporal presents the fullness of the gospel; the sanctoral exhibits those who have received the gospel in fullness. The temporal presents the medicine of immortality; the sanctoral offers case studies of those who have been forever cured. The temporal proclaims the way of holiness; the sanctoral displays heroes of holiness.

Following is a brief overview of the church calendar.

Advent

Advent, at least since the tenth century, has signaled the kick-off of the Christian year. The new year, liturgically speaking, doesn't begin on January 1; it begins in late November or early December with the first Sunday of Advent, four Sundays before December 25 (the Feast of the Nativity).

Advent is from the Latin equivalent of the Greek word *parousia*, which means "coming," "appearance" or "presence." It refers to the arrival of the king on an official visit.[14] This season initially focuses not on Christ's birth but on the final coming of Christ as Lord and Judge at the close of history, the end of all calendars. So Advent calls us to reflect on the end from the beginning. On the third Sunday of Advent, named *Gaudete* (Latin for "joyful"), Bethlehem comes into view, and from December 17 to 24 we joyfully anticipate the solemnity of Christmas, December 25.

Through Advent Christians wait, watch and hope in jubilant expectation. We must be ready for his coming, so we examine our consciences. Advent asks us, have we been lulled to spiritual sleep by the monotonous routines of this world's daily demands? Have we squandered our time in unworthy activities? Can we invest more of our time in acts of mercy, justice and conversion of souls? "You know what hour it is, how it is full time now for you to wake from sleep. For salvation is nearer to us now than when we first believed" (Romans 13:11).

Christmas

The Christmas season doesn't begin with Advent but with the Nativity of our Lord, December 25, and it lasts until the Baptism of the Lord on the third Sunday after Christmas Day. On December 28 the Feast of the Holy Innocents remembers the children martyred by Herod (see Matthew 2:16–18). On the Sunday within the octave of Christmas the Feast of the Holy Family holds forth the family of Jesus, Mary and Joseph as model of the virtues necessary for our families, the "domestic church." On January 1 we observe the Solemnity of Mary the Mother of God. On the following Sunday we rejoice in the Solemnity of the Epiphany, the manifestation (Greek *epiphaneia*) of Christ to all the nations (see Matthew 2:1–12). On the Sunday after the Epiphany the Christmas season concludes with the Feast of the Baptism of the Lord (see Matthew 3:13–16; Mark 1:9–11; Luke 3:21–22).

Ordinary Time 1

After the Christmas season we have a period called "Ordinary Time 1," which continues until the day before Ash Wednesday.

There is nothing ordinary about ordinary time. It is a time to catch our breath, consolidate our insights and integrate some of the lessons and experiences of Advent and the Christmas season. The Scripture readings focus on the life of Christ between his birth and his death and resurrection.

Lent

Lent is a penitential season of six Sundays and forty weekdays, beginning on Ash Wednesday. Ash Wednesday can be as early as February 4 and as late as March 11. The priest makes the sign of the cross with ashes on the foreheads of the faithful, a symbolic act of mourning over our sins.[15] "You are dust / to dust you shall return…. Repent, and believe in the gospel" are two phrases spoken as we receive the ashes (see Genesis 3:19; Mark 1:15).

Lent is a period of fasting, prayer and penance. Just as Jesus fasted forty days in the desert during his temptation by Satan (see Matthew 4:1–11; Luke 4:1–13) and Moses spent forty days fasting on Mount Sinai before the giving of the Ten Commandments (see Exodus 34:28), so Christians maintain this forty-day pattern of soul searching, fasting and repentance. These Lenten observances date back to the fourth century or earlier.

Holy Week and the Easter Triduum

Holy Week is the week before Easter Sunday. Palm Sunday recalls Jesus' triumphal entry into Jerusalem the week before his death (see Matthew 21:1–9; Mark 11:1–10; Luke 19:28–38; John 12:12–15). Even though this week after Palm Sunday is called Holy Week, Lent extends until the evening Mass on Holy Thursday.

Then begins the Triduum, the "space of three days" immediately before Easter. The Easter Triduum is the most sacred series of observances throughout the liturgical year. It begins with the evening "Mass of the Lord's Supper" on Holy Thursday, continues through Good Friday and Holy Saturday, climaxes in the Easter Vigil and concludes with the Evening Prayer of Easter Sunday.

Holy Thursday sometimes is called "Maundy Thursday" because it commemorates Jesus' *mandate,* command, to his apostles in the Upper Room to love one another and to demonstrate it by washing one another's feet. The "Mass of the Lord's Supper" also memorializes the institution of the priesthood, by which Christ's sacrifice is continued in the world (see John 13:1–17, 34).

The next day we observe the passion and death of Jesus. The Good Friday liturgy is very moving, with a dramatic reading of the arrest, trial, crucifixion and burial of Christ, along with the veneration of the cross. So somber is the mood that it is the only day of the year in which the Mass is not celebrated.

The second day of the Triduum technically begins at sunset on Good Friday and goes until sunset on Holy Saturday. It represents the burial of Jesus. Holy Saturday is a day of preparation for the Easter festival.

The third day of the Triduum begins at sunset on Holy Saturday with the Easter Vigil, which is a nocturnal watch for Christ's victorious emergence from the tomb as our resurrected Lord. Saint Augustine called it "the mother of all vigils," and it climaxes the liturgical year. Words cannot do it justice. The readings proclaim the full range of salvation history; all people in the entire congregation renew their baptismal promises, invoke the saints and renounce Satan; baptisms and confirmations occur.

Listing the component parts utterly fails to convey the glory of the Resurrection palpably present in this festivity. The Easter Vigil cannot be told; it must be shown. Our passage from death to life through the resurrection of Christ is presented in stunning worship and majestic liturgy, in full accord with the glory of the event.

The Easter Season

Easter is a season, not just a Sunday. We should think of the Sundays between Easter and Pentecost as Sundays "of," not "after," Easter.

The feast of Easter itself lasts eight days, called the "Octave of Easter." The eight-day observance stems from the early church's belief that the Resurrection inaugurates the "eighth" day of creation, the first day of the new creation. The original six days of creation had been capped with the Sabbath day of rest, a sign of the old covenant. Further, history itself extended through seven eras or "days," and now, on the eighth day, a new age, a new creation, a new covenant commenced.[16]

Ascension Thursday, forty days after Easter, recalls Christ's physical departure from this earth (see Acts 1:9). Upon his parting begins a novena (nine days of prayer), imitating the disciples and Mary as they waited for the promised Holy Spirit (see Acts 1:8, 12–14). On Pentecost (Greek for *fiftieth*) the Spirit is poured out on all flesh (see Acts 2). The church is now prepared to proclaim the word of God with power. With Christ physically in heaven and his Spirit extending his presence on the earth, we enter Ordinary Time 2.

Ordinary Time 2

Ordinary Time 2 begins the day after Pentecost and ends on the Saturday before Advent. The overall purpose of the season is to elaborate the themes of salvation history, rather than present events in the life of Christ as in Ordinary Time 1. Ordinary Time 2 includes the solemnities of the Holy Trinity, the Body and Blood of Christ, the Sacred Heart, the Birth of John the Baptist, Saints Peter and Paul, the Assumption, All Saints' Day and Christ the King, the last Sunday of the liturgical year, which looks forward to the time when God will be all in all (see 1 Corinthians 15:28).

During the liturgical year local bishops can and should designate particular days or periods of prayer for the harvest, human rights and equality, justice and peace, and penitential observance outside of Lent. The practice of declaring particular days of prayer and fasting is rooted in the Old Testament. No doubt the practice continued in the early church, although we currently have records tracing it back only to the third century.

Redeeming the calendar is one particularly beautiful and socially powerful way of declaring the priorities of the kingdom of God, even as we live in the kingdom of man. The "civilization of love" begins in the sacrificial death and resurrected glory of Christ. Christ remains with us body, blood, soul and divinity in the sacrament of the Eucharist. "Re-sacralizing" the temporal order means placing right worship at the center. Cult is the heart of culture, and the radiating center of the Resurrection expressed through the liturgical calendar is the beating heart of the cult.

What is the Liturgy of the Hours?

The Liturgy of the Hours is, first of all, a liturgy. The word *liturgy* is from the Greek *leitourgia,* meaning "work."[17] It is a work or action performed by a people in public, usually according to a prescribed ritual. Second, the Liturgy of the Hours is a highly organized cycle of psalms, hymns, songs, intercessory and petitioning prayers and readings from Scripture, the church fathers and the saints. All these elements are arranged to be communally prayed, chanted and read at scheduled hours of the day.

Some of the language associated with the Liturgy of the Hours warrants explanation. Sometimes it is called "The Divine Office," where *office* has the old meaning of "function, purpose or duty." It was the duty of clerics to pray it on behalf of the church. Sometimes it is called the "Breviary," which is from *abbreviation,* so called because a breviary is the book whose pages bring together all the elements.

Hours refers to a set time to assemble as the body of Christ and not a literal sixty minutes of prayer. Those unfamiliar with it might confuse it with the "Holy and Divine Liturgy" or the "Eucharistic Liturgy," most commonly known as "Holy Mass." But while in the Liturgy of the Hours we pray together as Christ's members with Christ, our Head, we don't celebrate a sacrament.

Sometimes it is just called "the Office" or "the Hours." "Liturgy of the Hours," however, is the preferred name, because after all, it is a liturgy, and the different parts of it are intended for different hours of the day.

This "prayer of the church" developed from the Jewish custom of praying at set times. "Seven times a day I praise thee," sings the psalmist (Psalm 119:164; see Daniel 6:10; Psalm 55:17). This practice combined with the apostolic command to "always...pray and not lose heart" (Luke 18:1; see Ephesians 6:18; Colossians 4:2; 1 Thessalonians 5:17). Even the most faithful, however, cannot dispense with all other responsibilities in order to pray all day. To do so wouldn't lead to "constant" but rather "chronic" prayer, and no doubt one's employer, wife and children would find such preoccupation toxic to their own lives and well-being. After all, for a Christian every undertaking is supposed to be a prayer.

While the Old Testament command to offer sacrifice in the morning and evening certainly influenced the Christian Liturgy of the Hours, scholars disagree over the degree of influence the many forms of first-century Judaism exerted on it. We do know that Jesus prayed in the morning (see Mark 1:35) and in the evening (Matthew 14:23; Mark 6:46–47) and kept vigil (Luke 6:12).

In the Acts of the Apostles we see the disciples praying at the third, sixth and ninth hours (see Acts 2:1, 15; 10:9; 3:1; 10:3, 30). We also know the disciples imitated Jesus in praying at night (Acts 16:25; 2 Corinthians 6:5). The idea of vigil shows up in the New Testament (see Matthew 25:1–13; Mark 13:33–37; Luke12:35–40; 1 Thessalonians 5:2; Revelation 3:3; 16:15). We also know that Christians had set psalms, hymns, readings and prayers in their gatherings (see 1 Corinthians 14:26; Ephesians 5:14–20; Colossians 3:16).

"The Christians of Pontus whom Pliny reported to the Emperor Trajan (c. 110) had a morning meeting which seems to have been nonsacramental, and an evening meal, which may have been an agape [a love feast], a Eucharist, or both."[18] Clear evidence of continuing nonsacramental public meetings is scanty and may depend on the extent to which Christians carried over synagogue practices into the second and third centuries.[19] From the second half of the fourth century, a Spanish nun named Egeria described a fully elaborated daily office. In the eighth and ninth centuries, however, what we commonly call the Liturgy of the Hours, divided into seven "hours," took fixed form in the monasteries and cathedrals.[20] There would be no major revision until 1971.

Not surprisingly, it was in the monasteries that these scheduled "hours" of prayer matured to the benefit of all the people of God.[21] Praying the Liturgy of the Hours allows us to find some fulfillment of the aspiration to praise God continuously and communally even if we aren't monks. In it we "sanctify time" by joining in Christ's intercessory prayers at the right hand of the Father, even as we remain immersed *in* the world *for* the world.

> The psalms are the song and prayer book of the Hours. To sing the psalms with understanding, then, is to meditate on them verse by verse, with the heart always ready to respond in the way the Holy Spirit desires. The one who inspired the psalmist will also be present to those who in faith and love are ready to receive his grace.... In praying the psalms we should open our hearts to the different attitudes they express...psalms of grief, trust, gratitude, etc.[22]

If one can manage to do all seven monastic hours, he or she will have prayed through all 150 psalms every two weeks. In 1971 a reform of the Office, the New Breviary, permitted the three daytime hours (terce, sext, none) to be collapsed into one daytime prayer, which still permits the entire Psalter to be sung in a four-week period.[23] In the reform the Liturgy of the Hours is now Morning, Daytime, Evening and Night Prayer.

The twin pillars and *sine qua non* of the Hours are Morning and Evening Prayer. "In keeping with the ancient tradition of the universal Church, Morning and Evening Prayer form a double hinge of the daily Office and are therefore to be considered the principal Hours and celebrated as such" (*Sacrosanctum Concilium,* 89).

The basic structure of each hour, with some variations, is

❖ a plea to God for assistance or a pledge to praise him

❖ an invitation to worship and a hymn

❖ antiphonal (Latin, *antiphone,* "counter sound") chanting of psalms

❖ readings from Scripture, the fathers and the saints

❖ in some hours a brief homily

❖ more psalms or the song of Mary (Luke 1:46–55), Simeon (1:68–79) or Zechariah (2:29–35)

❖ prayers with responses, intercessions, litanies and the Lord's Prayer

❖ dismissal

Various religious orders have their own breviaries, which differ somewhat from the one issued by Pope Paul VI. The following schedule is from the Abbey of Gethsemani in Trappist, Kentucky, where I first experienced the Liturgy of the Hours. It reflects the monastic rule of the Cistercian Order rather than the cathedral discipline. The commentary is mine.

3:15 A.M.: Mid-Night Prayer, known as Vigils. "At midnight there was a cry: 'Behold, the bridegroom! Come out to meet him.'... Watch, therefore—for you do not know when the master of the house will come, in the evening, or at midnight, or at cockcrow, or in the morning—lest he come suddenly and find you asleep" (Matthew 25:6; Mark 13:35–36).

5:45 A.M.: Morning Prayer, called Lauds, which means "praise." Appropriately, psalms of praise for creation and re-creation mark this dedication of the day to our God, Creator and Redeemer. We awaken and arise, urged on by the cosmic symbolism of a dawning new day, the traditional symbol of Christ's resurrection.

The Daytime Hours (Terce, Sext, None) focus on Psalms 120–132, the "songs of ascent." Old Testament scholars believe that these psalms were sung by worshippers as they climbed the stairs to the Jerusalem temple or by pilgrims as they climbed "up to Jerusalem," which sat on a hill, for annual religious festivals. Hippolytus (c. 170–c. 236), Tertullian (c. 160–c. 225) and Cyprian (d. 258) all recommend prayer at the third, sixth and ninth hours because of how these hours are connected to the crucifixion.

7:30 A.M.: Mid-Morning, known as Terce (Middle English for *third*), was considered the hour when Christ was nailed to the tree of the cross. Psalms 118–121 are chanted.

12:15 P.M.: Mid-Day, Sext (Middle English for *sixth*), the hour when Jesus was fastened to the cross (Psalms 122–124; 128–130).

2:15 P.M.: None, when blood and water flowed from Jesus' wounded side (Psalms 125–127; 131–132).

5:30 P.M.: Evening Prayer, Vespers (which means "evening"). "Let my prayer be counted as incense before thee, and the lifting up of my hands as an evening sacrifice" (Psalm 141:2) became a favorite psalm and prompted the burning of sweet-smelling incense as a symbol of Christ's sacrifice on Calvary. Vespers is, then, the evening sacrifice of praise and thanksgiving for Christ, our light in a darkening world. Psalms 109–144 are commonly used. The *Magnificat* is the climax of the hour, and the church thanks God for his might and mercy.

7:30 P.M.: Night Prayer is known as Compline (from the Latin word *completa,* meaning "complete"). These prayers before retiring (Psalms 4; 91; 134) are meditative. Compline concludes with an antiphon sung in honor of the Virgin Mother of God. Sleep is our daily rehearsal for death. Compline trains us to face it with profound trust in the protecting presence of Christ. The Song of Simeon, "Lord, now lettest thou thy servant depart in peace," is also sung (Luke 2:29–32).

Who should pray the Liturgy of the Hours? It is the "prayer of the church," the public prayer of the whole people of God, so it is for just about everyone. The General Instruction on the Liturgy of the Hours recommends it for parishes, groups of the faithful, sacred ministers and all clerics, bishops, priests, permanent deacons, religious communities of either sex, monks, nuns, canons, gatherings of the laity, members of any institute of perfection and families. Certain of these groups are mandated to pray the Liturgy of the Hours (see canon 276:2:3).

Since it is a "liturgy"—that is, a work of the people—it is best to do it with others. Don't let the best become the enemy of the good, however. Praying it alone is far preferable to not praying it at all. Various editions are available.[24]

When we pray the Liturgy of the Hours, the church acts in the priestly and intercessory role of Jesus. Pope Paul VI stated:

> This prayer takes its unity from the heart of Christ, for our Redeemer desired "that the life he had entered upon in his mortal body with supplications and with his sacrifice should continue without interruption through the ages in his Mystical Body, which is the Church." Because of this, the prayer of the Church is at the same time "the very prayer that Christ himself, together with his Body, addresses to the Father." As we celebrate the office, therefore, we must recognize our own voices echoing in Christ, his voice echoing in us.[25]

Our prayer resonates in Christ; his prayer resonates in us. The Liturgy of the Hours is, thus, a canticle of divine praise sung by Christ Jesus through his body, the church, and resounding in the halls of heaven.

Part IV
Hell

Why do Catholics believe in hell?

A few years ago a cover story from *U.S. News and World Report* caught my eye: "Hell Hath No Fury." A highlight stated, "With fire and brimstone out of fashion, modern thinking says the netherworld isn't so hot after all."[1]

With all due respect to modern thinking, I'm not surprised. Modern "thinking" is usually modern "feeling," and the doctrine of hell surely burns away any warm fuzzies. Indeed, the possibility of hell is meant to jolt my sensibilities, not console them. If the thought of everlasting torment doesn't trouble you, you haven't really weighed it seriously.

Hell is the state, place or condition of everlasting punishment for the unrepentant, those who die in a state of mortal sin, cut off from the grace of God. "God predestines no one to go to hell; for this, a willful turning away from God (a mortal sin) is necessary, and persistence in it until the end" (*CCC*, #1037).[2] Mortal sins are so grave, when deliberate and undertaken with full knowledge, that they kill the life of God within us. While the church has never officially taught that anyone is actually in hell,[3] it seems likely that hell will have human residents.

Pope John Paul II, respecting both the holiness of God and the conscience of man, stressed that no man has the authority to dismiss any individual as finally unrepentant. "The silence of the Church is, therefore, the only appropriate position for Christian faith. Even when Jesus says of Judas, the traitor, 'It would be better for that man if he had never been born' (Mt 26:24), His words do not allude for certain to eternal damnation."[4]

Neither has the church defined the metaphysical nature of the pains and fire of hell.

We are certain, however, that God "desires all men to be saved and to come to the knowledge of the truth. For there is one God, and there is one mediator between God and men, the man Christ Jesus" (1 Timothy 2:4–6). Though Christ has given himself for all, not all receive the redemption that he secured and now offers. "He who believes and is baptized will be saved; but he who does not believe will be condemned" (Mark 16:16).

If I had dreamed up the Catholic faith, one of my first revisions upon awakening would be to repress the nightmare of hell. That my choices can reverberate through eternity and permanently land me in everlasting suffering burdens me with an awful responsibility. Much easier to flee freedom, forget mortality and snicker at the prospects of my eternal significance. T.S. Elliot observed that we humans have a hard time coming to grips with reality.[5]

But it won't do to recoil in horror and fashion a less demanding version of Christianity. Jesus apparently didn't want it that way, since the most frightening words about possible damnation are found on his lips: "Depart from me, you cursed, into the eternal fire prepared for the devil and his angels" (Matthew 25:41).

According to the Gospels, hell is "unquenchable fire," "the furnace of fire," where the "worm does not die" and "the fire is not quenched" (Matthew 3:12; 13:42; Mark 9:43, 48; Matthew 5:22; 18:9). In hell you would "weep and gnash your teeth" in "outer darkness" (Luke 13:28; Matthew 8:12; see 2 Peter 2:17; Jude 13). Pope Benedict XVI wrote: "The idea of eternal damnation, which had taken ever clearer shape in the Judaism of the century or two before Christ, has a firm place in the teaching of Jesus, as well as in the apostolic writings. Dogma takes its stand on solid ground when it speaks of the existence of Hell and of the eternity of its punishments."[6]

Some try to soften the menacing language by calling it symbolic. Symbolic it certainly is. Fire and darkness can't literally coexist at the same time in the same place. But Jesus strains the limits of language because the reality surpasses the symbol in horror. Just as heaven is beyond our dreams, so is hell worse than can be imagined.

There is no denying that throughout his preaching, Jesus set forth only two final possibilities for human beings. One is everlasting happiness in the presence of God, the other everlasting torment in the absence of God. We can reject this doctrine as false, but we can't claim Christ didn't teach it.

*H*ow can a person knowingly choose hell?

As illogical as it sounds, some people do choose hell. This intuition appears in Western legends, novels, poetry, operas and songs that depict a person who sells his or her soul to the devil. The human soon forgets the bargain, as life grows full of success, comfort and indulgence, and is lulled into believing that the deal was all a fantasy. But the devil returns on the appointed day to claim the soul he bought years before.

The Faust legend has been treated by some of the Western world's greatest writers and composers. Legendary blues musician Robert Johnson capitalized on the story that he had "gone down to the crossroads" and sold his soul to the devil in order to play guitar better than anyone else. But does a decisive choice of evil in "real" life make any sense?[7]

What could possibly qualify as a motive for such a choice? As long as the person's will is hampered by ignorance, deception or bondage to desire, isn't God's grace able to transform the sinner without meddling with human freedom? Can't God loosen those sinister influences on the will so that the person is returned to a moment of true freedom to choose the good? And once a human will is "free," what motive remains for choosing eternal misery for oneself?

After all, isn't God "forbearing toward you, not wishing that any should perish, but that all should reach repentance" (2 Peter 3:9)? Yes, he is, but do people choose evil when they know better? The Christian answer, through tears, is yes. Just as the journey of a thousand miles begins with one step, so does the road to hell get laid down brick by brick.

A person renders himself fit for damnation by developing a taste for evil. The "damned" exhibit a consistency of character. They have become the sum of what they have chosen. Their identities are now frozen as the sexually immoral, thieves, drunkards and so forth (see 1 Corinthians 6:9–10).

In his diary Joseph Goebbels (1897–1945), the Nazi propaganda master, reacted to viewing some newsreel footage showing the German army's devastation of Poland. He had determined that it was good to destroy Poland. Nevertheless, as he viewed the newsreel, he found his desire for destruction weakening. He forced himself forward with the words, "Be hard, my heart, be hard."[8]

The ultimate judgment is God's, and we should never presume that any person is beyond redemption (not even Nazis). But in this instance aren't we witnessing the crystallizing of a heart cast in evil? Goebbels had to guard against the temptation to choose, even desire, good in the same way that a Saint Francis had to guard against the temptation to choose evil.

You're excused for thinking, "Hell must require spectacular evil, and spectacular evil seems so much like the Nazis, and the

Nazis seem so unlike the rest of us that the Goebbels example misses the mark." But does it?

The racist hubris behind the Holocaust has come to function in popular discussion as a substitute for the devil's poisoned fruit. It has displaced the "talking serpent" as the West's icon of barbarity. For all the books and films that deal with it, however, it has become as unreal, remote, even as mythic as the satanic encounter with the Man and the Woman. As such it has become hard to believe that such evil choices remain living options for unexceptional, ordinary people in spite of Hannah Arendt's familiar phrase, "the banality of evil."[9]

So Nazi atrocities have become the gold standard against which moral evil is gauged. Even those who pride themselves on not being judgmental are willing to issue moral judgments when it comes to the Nazis.

This same reflexive outrage bursts out against pedophiles, prolific serial killers, deadbeat dads, turbaned terrorists, incompetent surgeons and smokers in a restaurant's non-smoking section. We loathe these transgressors because we're convinced we couldn't be such cads, sociopaths and moral lepers. Satan may be unconvincing as the ideal exemplar of personal evil, but Hitler and Ted Bundy still function for us quite nicely because they are the "not me."

The teaching of Judaism and Christianity is, however, that we are capable of becoming real Goebbelses and Bundys. It is through ordinary individuals that the unthinkable becomes normalized. From the Armenian genocide at the beginning of the last century through the two World Wars, the holocaust of the Jews, Stalin's purges, Mao's revolutionary violence, the savagery of the Khmer Rouge, the Rwandan genocide and the current threat of nuclear terrorism, the last century has been the bloodiest century in known history. All these horrific acts occurred with the active or passive cooperation of normal, decent people like me. So I ask: What evils have I become acclimated to by my tacit acceptance or half-conscious planning?

With each moral decision we are forming the selves that will persist for eternity. We will be wonders to behold or horrors from whom we flee in revulsion. "To have a self, to be a self, is the greatest concession made to man, but at the same time it is eternity's demand upon him."[10]

Psychiatrist M. Scott Peck noted that certain otherwise unremarkable patients "have crossed the line and descended into 'radical,' likely inescapable evil." These people are not defined by the magnitude of their evil but "by the consistency of their sins. While usually subtle, their destructiveness is remarkably consistent. This is because those who have 'crossed over the line' are characterized by their *absolute* refusal to tolerate the sense of their own sinfulness."[11] They grow to love wickedness.

It is possible that a man will let himself be so mastered by his desires or indifference that he will "lose all ability to master his desires or rouse his will to virtue. It is the extreme case of what we have all too often seen: people increasingly mastered by desires, so that they lose some of their ability to resist them. The less we impose our order on our desires, the more they impose their order on us. We may describe a man in this situation as having 'lost his soul.'"[12] Columbine High School mass murderer, a suburban teen, Eric Harris, with no obvious evidence of abuse, psychosis or grievance, wrote, "I'm full of hate and I love it. I hate people and they better…fear me."[13]

With most of us there are no spectacular sins, just an undistinguished mediocrity, a dimming of our desire to seek and serve God, a subtle bending of our will in the direction of self-indulgence that, if allowed to go on forever, would bury us under a suffocating and overpowering excess. As C.S. Lewis's senior tempter, Screwtape, advises his demonic protégé on how best to seduce a human soul to damnation: "Murder is no better than cards if cards can do the trick. Indeed the safest road to Hell is the gradual one—the gentle slope, soft underfoot, without sudden turnings, without milestones, without signposts."[14]

Sometimes things are too close to be seen. Our old familiar selves with ingrained responses, acquired associations, filtered perceptions and rationalized motivations need to be shaken up and driven to reexamine our relationships and our consciences. How difficult it is to stay awake and make our decisions in the light of eternity. The ordinary rhythms and rituals of everyday life often anesthetize us to the possibilities of damnation or beatitude. People preoccupied with the affairs of this world excuse *themselves* from the feast that is symbolic of salvation (see Luke 14:16–24; Matthew 22:1–14).

"As were the days of Noah, so will be the coming of the Son of man. For as in those days before the flood they were eating and drinking, marrying and giving in marriage, until the day when Noah entered the ark, and they did not know until the flood came and swept them all away, so will be the coming of the Son of man" (Matthew 24:37–39; see also Romans 2:8–9; 2 Thessalonians 1:9; Jude 7).

The flow of daily life blinded Noah's generation to their sin and spiritual indifference. Do those of us born into the bloodiest century in human history, the first barraged by the stimuli of electronic media and marked like no other by the license to consume and accumulate more than any previous generation, really believe that we exceed the moral sensitivity of Noah's contemporaries? Jesus jolts us with the warning that it is better to cut off a limb or pluck out an eye, if either lures us into sin, than to enter hellfire with all our members intact (see Matthew 5:29–30). Jesus is not encouraging self-mutilation but making the point that sin must be dealt with drastically, even "surgically."

This prospect of eternity turns our ordinary activities of life into moments of great significance.

> Everything nudges our elbow. Heaven and Hell seem to lurk under every bush. The sarcastic lift of an eyebrow carries the seed of murder, since it bespeaks my wish to diminish someone else's existence. To open a door for a man carrying luggage recalls the Cross, since it is a small case in point of putting the other person first. We live in the middle of all of this, but it is so routine that it is hard to stay alive to it. The prophets and poets have to pluck our sleeves or knock us on the head now and again, not to tell us anything new but simply to hail us with what has been there all along.[15]

All the "damnation sayings" of Jesus are calculated to sensitize our conscience and persuade us of hell's existence and the possibility that any of us may end up there. He warns in love. Neighbors who stand mute when they see smoke wafting from your attic, doctors who withhold your true condition from you, priests and ministers who omit hell from their sermons, only imagine that their timid silence is love. They are false friends, bad neighbors and unfaithful ministers. The Catholic church is duty-bound to preserve the understanding of life Jesus taught. Even if some preaching "scares the hell out of us," its aim is to scare us out of hell.

In one sense, people don't choose hell any more than a young alcoholic chooses cirrhosis. The seven deadly sins are called "deadly" not because they immediately and overtly crush the perpetrator. But because they eventually steal the life from him or her. Ultimately, choosing hell is about countless turnings from God's life until I've come to enjoy averting my gaze.

The person who has learned to perpetually turn from God is like the kid who enjoys spinning around and getting dizzy. At first there is a heady excitement, a novel and "dynamic" perspective, but eventually he is cast from the center of the stable world and distanced from reality. Just as the whirling child is engulfed in sensations of isolation, waves of nausea and the inability to orient, so go those who defy or ignore God, the ultimate reality, and try to spin a world of their own imagining. Rather than become the gods of their worlds, they become the slaves of their own vertigo.

Why can't all people go to heaven?

I remember swimming with an elder of a church I once attended. As we relaxed in his pool, he asked me if I believed in hell. I told him that I did but wouldn't mind finding a way out of it.

He laughed, looked around and told me, as though he were a schoolboy about to share a secret crush, that he believed that after death, there would be a moment when people met Jesus Christ in all his glory and were asked, "Do you love me?" People fearful of judgment would be so relieved and exclaim, "Lord, you know that I love you." Ultimately, he said, all would be forever with Jesus.

My friend assumed that people die still capable of repentance. He was a good man, great fun and no mean student of Scripture—and he was a "universalist." He believed all would be saved. Many people share his sentiments if not his postmortem scenario.

There are many "universalisms," some good, some bad. One universalism opines that the door out of hell is only locked on the inside. Then there is a universalism that presumes that "Jesus is just all right with me," and everyone is just all right with Jesus, so everything is just going to turn out OK.

Then there is the historic Christian universalism, which teaches that every person *without exception* is worthy of respect because he or she is created in the image and likeness of God. *Everyone* can be transformed and become a coheir with Christ, a royal priest, a child of God. Further, the gospel is to be preached in *all* the world, to *all* peoples. In Christ "there is neither Jew nor Greek, there is neither slave nor free, there is neither male nor female" (Galatians 3:28; see also Romans 10:12; 1 Corinthians 12:13; Ephesians 2:15–18). Historic Christian "universalism" insists that all *types* of people will be saved. But not *all* people, without exception, will spend eternity with God.

Saint Catherine of Genoa wrote of God's love that "every pleasure, when compared to it, is pain, and such riches does it confer on a man, that all beside should seem to him but misery."[16] Who can resist his love? Jesus, however, knew that people do reject the love of God. He lamented, "O Jerusalem, Jerusalem, killing the prophets and stoning those who are sent to you! How often would I have gathered your children together as a hen gathers her brood under her wings, and you would not!" (Matthew 23:37–39; see also John 5:40). *"You would not!"* Those are the three most poignant words in Scripture.

Jesus' desire to gather his people recalls the image of God sheltering his people under his wings (see Exodus 19:4; Deuteronomy 32:11; Psalm 17:8; 36:7; 63:7; 91:4). But as so often in the Old Testament, Jesus' love for Jerusalem gives way to the brokenhearted pain of their rejection.

It can't be stressed too much that the anguished heart of God, the grieving parent, seeks to win over his wayward child. God weeps over his judgment of Israel (see Jeremiah 8:21–22; 9:1, 10), though Israel had killed and persecuted his prophets

111

(see Jeremiah 26:20–23; 2 Chronicles 25:15–16; Isaiah 30:9–11; Amos 2:12).

From the cross Jesus' arms are outstretched to gather up the entire race and reconstitute the universal human family in his embrace. Not everyone, however, will consent to this embrace. What's a Lover to do?

> If the happiness of a creature lies in self-surrender, no one can make that surrender but himself (though many can help him to make it) and he may refuse. I would pay any price to be able to say truthfully "All will be saved." But my reason retorts, "Without their will, or with it?" If I say "Without their will" I at once perceive a contradiction; how can the supreme voluntary act of self-surrender be involuntary? If I say "With their will," my reason replies "How if they *will not* give in?"[17]

God cannot save all persons except by reducing the resistors to non-persons—that is, by refusing to respect their will. When all opportunities for repentance have passed and all divine and human appeals are exhausted, we are still left with a person who must choose for himself or herself. "In the famous painting of Jesus with a lamp knocking on a door (= your soul), there is no knob on the outside of the door. Only from the inside can the door be opened, freely, to goodness and truth and joy. And only from the inside can it be locked. If we lock that door, our folly and crime is its own punishments."[18]

Why can't God break the resistant will of the soul by overwhelming it with the grace of repentance? Why can't God simply annihilate it and put it out of its eternal misery? God can do neither of these things because they are absurd. It is as impossible for God to save persons by making them non-persons as it is for him to make a rock so big he can't lift it. He can no more annihilate an immortal soul than he can lie or make three plus two equal eight. Miracles are a gesture in God's repertoire; nonsense is not.

> When all that is now hidden is revealed, we shall see that to convert or annihilate a lost soul would involve an absurdity comparable to that of constructing a square circle. In this present life, we can see clearly that a figure ceases to be a circle if it is transformed into a square. After death, we shall see that God's release or annihilation of a lost soul would demand such a change in Him that He would cease to be God. For God has pledged Himself not to deprive man of his liberty and existence, even if he misuses these gifts. God in His justice will not destroy the integrity of human choice.[19]

Ironically, to believe that all human beings can be saved by a simple divine decree debases rather than elevates the human person. Think about your efforts to win people over to your love or your cause. Granted, compared to the deity or Dale Carnegie, we all fall short of winning friends and influencing people. But since a person's will is a holy of holies, no one, not even God, can enter it by force without defiling it.

Neither God nor anyone else can compel someone's agreement or love through overwhelming force. That would be rape not love, exploitation not cooperation—and God's character is at least as benign as the proverbial English gentleman's. "Dehumanize the human so we can save him" deserves a place in Orwell's *1984*. It is simply doublespeak. "Hell is one of the eternal guarantees of human freedom, for it admits the right of a free man to cry out *non-serviam* through all eternity."[20] In Milton's *Paradise Lost* Lucifer would rather revolt against heaven than serve there; at least in hell he can be king.[21]

The eighteenth-century British evangelist John Wesley speaks for the vast majority of Christians when he writes that God's goodness is displayed most clearly "in offering salvation to every creature, actually saving all that consent thereto, and doing for the rest all that infinite wisdom, almighty power, and boundless love can do, without forcing them to be saved, which would be to destroy the very nature that he had given them."[22]

*I*sn't hell a bit of overkill?

Some people feel that the penalty doesn't fit the crime. My response may sound cryptic: God is infinite; we are immortal; love takes two.

By nature we both (God and man) last forever and ever. The big question is, "Will love keep us together?" Given our natures, an eternal hell must be a possible outcome.

The Nature of God

The maxim is sound: Let the punishment fit the crime. But God is not, first of all, a judge, and we aren't, first of all, criminals. He is a Father, and we are his children. Hell is primarily a consequence of human character rather than a sentence handed down by a judge.

Pope John Paul II took great care to emphasize that "damnation consists precisely in definitive separation from God, freely chosen by the human person and confirmed with death that seals his choice for ever. God's judgment ratifies this state."[23] Souls choose hell by refusing divine love. God's judgment simply acknowledges the fact of that refusal. But how can it be fair for an offense committed by a finite person in time to receive an eternal punishment from an infinite person?

To begin we must note that crimes against animals, property and persons all differ in respect to their penalties. Even within the category of human persons, we find the severity of the crime is sometimes gauged according to the person it is committed against. Although we have become a far more egalitarian society than during the days of monarchy and empire, we still treat an attempted murder of a president with greater severity than the attempted murder of a "common" person.

But even if we recognized no distinction among human persons, we find ourselves on different ground with God. A crime against God is a crime against not only a person but a person who is of a higher order of being, an infinite person. In fact, he is the source of all being. Sin against an infinite God is an infinite sin worthy of infinite punishment. As Saint Thomas Aquinas wrote: "The magnitude of the punishment matches the magnitude of the sin.... Now a sin that is against God is infinite; the higher the person against whom it is committed, the graver the sin—it is more criminal to strike a head of state than a private citizen—and God is of infinite greatness. Therefore, an infinite punishment is deserved for a sin committed against him."[24]

The Nature of Man

Now we move to our nature. Because we are immortal souls designed to live forever, our eternal destiny depends on our relationship to the eternal God who created us in his image.

Sometimes we get the impression that our standing with God is more a matter of rules than relationship, that our covenant with God is like a contract with an employer or that we are criminals transgressing a code rather than sons rebelling against a Father.

So God is not, first of all, a judge. In fact, most of his judgments sound like the laments of a spurned lover. "Surely, as a faithless wife leaves her husband, so have you been faithless to me, O house of Israel, says the LORD" (Jeremiah 3:20; see also 31:32; Hosea 2:16–17). This spousal love between God and his people is testified to throughout both the Old and New Testaments.[25]

God places the soul in hell by the very act of being himself, of being Absolute Goodness and Love in the face of a soul who rejects goodness and love. Similarly, the damned place themselves in hell by the very act of being themselves, of being people who have deliberately excluded the love of God from their lives. Once again C.S. Lewis puts it so succinctly: "The damned...enjoy forever the horrible freedom they have demanded, and are therefore self-enslaved."[26]

God is the ultimate reality whose presence cannot be avoided, so those who seek some cosmic crevice in which to hide are doomed to futility. He's everywhere. The damned may have forsaken communion with God, but they have not lost their awareness of what they've lost. "The chief punishment of hell is eternal separation from God, in whom alone man can possess the life and happiness for which he was created and for which he longs" (*CCC,* #1035).

What about a second chance after death?

All the major streams of Christian tradition—Catholic, Anglican, Lutheran, Eastern Orthodox, Reformed, Anabaptist—agree that with death all possibility of conversion ends. *Human repentance requires the union of body and soul.* Now is the opportunity for redemption; death is the hour of reckoning. "It is appointed for men to die once, and after that comes judgment" (Hebrews 9:27).

Contrary to popular folk religion, purgatory is not a second chance. Those in purgatory are already "saved" and destined for heaven. Purgatory is simply the temporary place, state, condition or process after death by which those who are in Christ are purged of disordered self-love and cleansed of remaining moral and spiritual imperfections. "All who die in God's grace and friendship, but still imperfectly purified, are indeed assured of their eternal salvation; but after death they undergo purification, so as to achieve the holiness necessary to enter the joy of heaven" (*CCC*, #1030; see also 1 Corinthians 3:12–15).[27]

We can rest assured that if someone is reformable, he is alive. For God, who is immeasurable in mercy and impeccable in justice, will not allow anyone to go to hell whom he knew would go to heaven if he gave them more opportunity. Those who seek find, and those who ask receive, and for those who knock the door swings open, since it is only locked from the inside. Hell is only for the unrepentant and the reprobate (see 2 Peter 2:1–10).

If hell seems like overkill, then perhaps we underestimate the gravity of breaking faith with our Creator and Sustainer.

In Scripture God often imposed penalties that seemed disproportionate. Lot's wife became a pillar of salt because she looked back at Sodom and Gomorrah (Genesis 19:26). Nadab and Abihu fell dead for offering "unholy fire before the Lord in the wilderness" (Numbers 3:4; see also Leviticus 10:1–2). Moses was denied entry to the Promised Land because he struck the rock twice instead of speaking to it as God had commanded (Numbers 20:11). And in the early church God struck Ananias and Sapphira dead because they lied to the apostles about some property (Acts 5:1–10).

> [Scripture] views sin as an attack on God's character and therefore deserving of great punishment. Because Adam ate the forbidden fruit, he plunged the human race into sin with all of its terrible consequences. Paul writes with reference to Adam's sin: "The many died by the trespass of the one man.... The judgment followed one sin and brought condemnation.... By the trespass of the one man, death reigned through that one man.... The result of one trespass was condemnation for all men.... Through the

disobedience of the one man the many were made sinners"
(Rom 5:15–19).[28]

We are not the best judges of how our sin shatters God's
design and harms others.

People often object that they don't know anyone deserving
of hell. Good, but that is not my or your judgment to make. I
don't condemn or canonize anyone. My responsibility is to
present the Good News. Only God knows a person's inner
direction at any given moment. Only God is capable of weighing the varying influences of heredity, upbringing, temperament, geography and free choices that form us as persons.
"Although we can judge that an act is in itself a grave offense,
we must entrust judgment of persons to the justice and mercy
of God" (*CCC,* #1861).

Saint Paul tells us that God, like a father with a wayward
adult child, knows when the time has come to turn the disobedient over to their own selfish indulgences. God allows the
wrongdoing to run its course as an act of judgment, and spiritual deterioration intensifies. What follows are acts of moral
mayhem, including murder, strife, covetousness, gossip, hatred
of God, disobedience to parents, sexual deviance. To cap it off,
God gives them over to a reprobate mind, to do those things
that are not proper (see Romans 1:24, 26, 28). They have, as
Kierkegaard put it, "fulfilled their personalities in the despair of
defiance."[29]

Of course, hell doesn't fulfill but frustrates our humanity.
Souls created for glory melt like wax figures in the tropic sun,
their features disfigured beyond recognition. Men and women
warped by bad choices deteriorate into ruined remnants, the
skeletal remains of an abandoned edifice. The beatific project
remains forever in disrepair. The damned are barred from the
source of life and hope.

Scripture identifies those on the road to exclusion from God as "hardhearted" and "stiff-necked," the very opposite of contrite or brokenhearted. Believers are warned not to "harden" their hearts (see Psalm 95:8; Proverbs 28:14; Ephesians 4:18; Hebrews 3:8). The impression is that of a personality who has resolved to steel himself against the motions of God's grace. With each refusal of God's grace, another layer of scar tissue forms over the heart. With each rejection of God's will, the person bends away from God. As the heart cools toward God, the identity freezes and the person grows morally paralyzed.

This is judgment. Such a person simply remains his worst self, if there is any center to his identity at all. "Let the evildoer still do evil, and the filthy still be filthy" (Revelation 22:11).

In the long run many objections to the doctrine of hell are clarified with a question: "What are you asking God to do? To wipe out their past sins [of the damned] and, at all costs, to give them a fresh start, smoothing every difficulty and offering every miraculous help? But He has done so, on Calvary. To forgive them? They will not be forgiven. To leave them alone? Alas, I am afraid that is what He does."[30]

The tragic irony is that hell is not, first of all, imposed from outside ourselves; it is chosen from within ourselves. After all, God's desire is for all human beings to be saved and come to a knowledge of the truth (see 1 Timothy 2:4; 1 Thessalonians 5:9). He has created no one for hell but everyone for eternal friendship with him.

> We cannot be united with God unless we freely choose to love him. But we cannot love God if we sin gravely against him, against our neighbor or against ourselves.... Our Lord warns us that we shall be separated from him if we fail to meet the serious needs of the poor and the little ones who are his brethren. To die in mortal sin without repenting and accepting God's merciful love means remaining separated from him for ever by our own free choice.

> This state of definitive self-exclusion from communion with God and the blessed is called "hell." (*CCC*, #1033)

Love requires real freedom, and real freedom must include freedom to refuse God and damn oneself. As George MacDonald so gravely stated, "The one principle of hell is—'I am my own.'"[31] Or as Fulton J. Sheen wrote: "Why do souls go to hell?... They refuse to love. Love pardons everything except one thing—refusal to love."[32] If hell seems a disproportionate consequence, we haven't yet grasped the significance of human choice or the momentousness of the human "project."

Wouldn't having loved ones in hell destroy the joy of those in heaven?

"How can there be a paradise for any, while it is hell for a mother if her child were in hell?" This thought has been voiced in the church and outside it. It assures that hell can serve no positive purpose. If it had a positive purpose, then those in heaven would rejoice in it and their happiness wouldn't be tarnished.

Here we come to a serious problem—not of logic but of imagination. It is easy enough to argue that hell does, after all, serve a positive purpose. In hell the wicked will be useful for demonstrating the perfect justice of God, while those in heaven display his mercy and love. Just as a barren tree is useful only for firewood, so the disobedient are only fuel for an eternal fire.

In a sense the damned themselves, having been created to image God, have refused the opportunity to reflect him. Thus they have stripped themselves of their humanity. They have defiled their nature. They have refused to bring their nature to fruition. They are the fig tree that produces no figs. They are good only to be chopped down and their dead wood consumed in the fiery furnace.

Given certain assumptions, all this is not unreasonable. Yet it sounds like Reinhard Heydrich, the architect of the "final solution," calculating how many eyeglasses, gold fillings and prosthetic limbs could be salvaged for industrial purposes from condemned Jews after the ovens were full. The cool logic of it chills the mother's heart. Isn't heaven the place where God wipes the tear from every eye, where mourning will be no more, neither crying nor pain? For the old order of things has passed away, and he who is seated on the throne proclaims, "I make all things new" (see Revelation 21:4–5).

Wouldn't the heart of the saint, perfected in Christlikeness, find hell an intolerable chamber of horrors from which people must be rescued if heaven is to be truly a place of bliss? Wouldn't those in heaven, whose capacity for solidarity exceeds our own, be even less capable of resting in the presence of human suffering?

This is exactly what I mean by the problem of imagination. We cannot project on those in heaven our attitudes and emotional responses. There are aspects of love that a couple who have just discovered one another cannot grasp until they enter the married state. Or to use an infelicitous analogy, the inmate who is in for life adjusts to prison life differently than the one who is serving three to five years.

We live in the time of choosing; the saints live in the time of realization. Possibility and probation form the existential climate in which we choose and act, while the saints enjoy an environment created by consummation and confirmation. The shift in point of view, you might say, is heavenly.

To illustrate the difference, look at Jesus. During the time of Israel's choice, he wept over the unwillingness of his people to embrace the will of God. On earth he invited people into fellowship with him, healed them, declared the paramount importance of seeking the kingdom of God, revealed the Father. But when he returns at the end of history, the time for lamentation will be over, as will the time of invitation. "I am…bringing my recompense, to repay every one for what he has done" (Revelation 22:12).

There is no hint of reluctance or melancholy in these words. To the contrary, the song of triumph rings throughout the Apocalypse. The saints fully united in Christ's body see the world through his eyes. Indeed, they praise him for his judgments (see Revelation 6:10; 16:5–7; 19:1–3). They have come to fully share his view of all things.

But truth be told, we just aren't there yet. We cannot be expected to exult in the separation of the sheep and the goats, especially since we are fond of so many goats whom we still hope will eventually sprout some wool. As the boy in *Angels in the Outfield* kept repeating, "It could happen."

And this should be our attitude. As long as anyone remains on the earth, the possibility of redemption is alive. This is why we don't judge anyone as to his or her ultimate destination. This is why the church has no list of names of those who are in hell. We must dare to act toward everyone we meet as though he will repent and receive the Good News. We must dare to believe that we are God's coworkers in all of this.

But that is now. We still await the final transformation. The experience of seeing the Lord upon his return will change us. "Beloved, we are God's children now; it does not yet appear what we shall be, but we know that when he appears we shall be like him, for we shall see him as he is" (1 John 3:2). This process of transformation has already begun, but it is not yet complete. "And every one who thus hopes in him purifies himself as he is pure" (1 John 3:3).

After his rhapsodic words on love, Saint Paul reminds us: "For now we see in a mirror dimly, but then face to face. Now I know in part; then I shall understand fully, even as I have been fully understood" (1 Corinthians 13:12). When we enter the eternal state and all things are fulfilled, our minds and hearts will be utterly conformed to ultimate reality.

The luminosity of the experience is described in Jesus' revelation to John: "I saw no temple in the city [the heavenly Jerusalem], for its temple is the Lord God the Almighty and the Lamb. And the city has no need of sun or moon to shine upon it, for the glory of God is its light, and its lamp is the Lamb" (Revelation 21:22–23). This is the light of final perspective

I am not claiming that this answers the question of how having loved ones in hell will affect us. But it does remind us that we will be encountering realities that we can't even fully imagine. Therefore, we shouldn't disregard this seismic shift in perspective as a means of consoling us when we consider the permanent state of the finally impenitent.

Even on earth Jesus taught that it might be necessary to leave mother, father, sister or brother to become his disciples (see Matthew 10:34–37; Luke 14:26). How much more so in the new heavens and earth, when people's choices have been fully realized and we have flowered into the persons we were created to be or have shriveled into the scag that not even a mother could love.

Now, these are just suggestive remarks to help solve the imaginative problem that started this chapter. Right now you are on earth, the era of possibility and probation. Knowing the destiny of those who suppress the light of God's truth, aren't you ready to do all you can to win them to Christ? Living as we do in the time when men and women can still decide their eternal destinies, we should be driven to perform the corporal and spiritual works of mercy. The prospect that those we love may spend eternity apart from God is intense motivation to share the gospel and to change our behavior so that we embody the good, the true and the beautiful.

I am consoled by remembering that the Holy Spirit is more at work, invisibly calling people, than the church is in its visible mission. No one who would have chosen differently if given another opportunity will be in hell. Even at the close of the Book of Revelation, after John has been shown the behind-the-scenes spiritual warfare that unfolds history, God issues an invitation. He does so to the very end of time: "The Spirit and the Bride say, 'Come.' And let him who hears say, 'Come.' And let him who is thirsty come, let him who desires take the water of life without price" (Revelation 22:17).

ᘯhy must hell last forever?

Occasionally someone will propose that hell is temporary until people repent and are rendered fit for heaven. In the end, they say, all will be united with God, although many may first have to suffer in hell.

Initially it's an attractive notion, but it distorts the Scriptural picture. Consider the separation of the sheep from the goats in Matthew 25. Christ, as judge, will first say, "'Come, O blessed of my Father, inherit the kingdom prepared for you from the foundation of the world.'... Then he will say to those at his left hand, 'Depart from me, you cursed, into the eternal fire prepared for the devil and his angels'" (Matthew 25:35, 41). "And they [the lost] will go away into eternal [*aionion*] punishment, but the righteous into eternal [*aionion*] life" (Matthew 25:46).

The same word that is used to describe the final condition of the unjust is used to describe the just. If hell is temporary, so too is heaven. Since there is no question about the endless duration of heaven, I'm compelled to say the same about hell.[33]

Occasionally someone will try and continue the argument by claiming that *aionios,* which usually is translated "forever" and "eternal," literally means "belonging to the age." So, emboldened with this bit of semantic subtlety, they reason that the word *eternal* can refer to the "spiritual quality" of the age rather than its "endless duration." Hell, they claim, ceases with the closing of the age in which repentance remained possible. Hell, in this view, is temporary. Eventually the unrepentant are annihilated. Those who hold this position also reject the immortality of the human soul.

First of all, "never in the New Testament are the words *Aion* or *Aionion* used of limited periods of time."[34] Saint Paul also draws a striking contrast: "The things that are seen are transient [*proskairos,* literally, 'for a season'], but the things that are unseen are eternal [*aionios*]" (2 Corinthians 4:18). Further, *aionios* is used of persons and things that are, by their very nature, endless: God, his power and glory, Christ's redemption, the salvation of human beings and Christ's future rule.[35]

Other forms of *aionios* indicate unending duration: "Jesus Christ is the same yesterday and today and for ever [*aionas*]" (Hebrews 13:8). The clear point of the passage is that Jesus Christ is, for now and all eternity, the same! Further, the twenty-four elders fall down before the eternal God and worship him who lives "for and ever"—that is, *aionas ton aionon*" (see Revelation 4:10; 10:6; 11:15).

Eternal is used sixty-four times to refer to the heavenly realities on the other side of death. In all cases it refers to duration without end. It may mean more than infinite duration, but it certainly doesn't mean less.

In a corresponding opposite Saint Paul uses *aionios* to refer to the retribution owed to the wicked: "They shall suffer the punishment of eternal destruction and exclusion from the presence of the Lord" (2 Thessalonians 1:9). The Revelation of Jesus to John compounds the point: "The smoke of their torment goes up for ever and ever.... They will be tormented day and night for ever and ever [*eis aionas aionon*]" (Revelation 14:11; 20:10). Realistically, hell is as irreversible as heaven.

Because we are immortal, we will be forever who we choose to be today. Eternity confirms what we have been in time.

> Christianity asserts that every individual human being is going to live forever, and this must be either true or false. Now there are a good many things which would not be worth bothering about if I were going to live only seventy years, but which I had better bother about very seriously if I am going to live for ever. Perhaps my bad temper or my jealousy are gradually getting worse—so gradually that the increase in seventy years will not be very noticeable. But it might be absolute hell in a million years: in fact, if Christianity is true, Hell is the precisely correct technical term for what it would be.[36]

The tragedy of hell is measured not in the duration of human suffering but in the distortion of the human person, not quantity of moments but quality of life. Strictly speaking, hell occurs outside of time, and the charge that it is overkill because of its duration misses the point.

We should think of hell as existing in another dimension than time, just as time is another dimension than space. What we make of ourselves in time and space—that is, in history— will be "fleshed out" in eternity, just as a piece of music composed on the piano can be transposed and "fleshed out" when it is arranged for orchestra. We hear a new dimension to the music.

Or if on earth we are squares, then we are cubes in eternity. "The relation between earthly choices and eternal rewards or punishments is not like the relation between crimes and prison sentences, but like the relation between a foundation and a building. It is not external but internal."[37] We amplify into eternity what we have become in time.

In the 1990 movie *Ghost,* Sam (Patrick Swayze) is killed during a botched mugging. His love for his partner, Molly (Demi Moore), enables him to remain in communion with her on earth even though he is a ghost. In one conversation through a medium (Whoopi Goldberg), he marvels over a feature of the afterlife: "It's amazing, Molly. The love inside: you take it with you." The reverse is also, sadly, true. The spiritual indifference or hostility or gluttony or greed inside takes you with it—right into eternity.

Isn't hell just a tool of manipulation and terror?

This question is a bit cynical, isn't it? The most admired and influential figure in the history of the world, he who summarized the whole of the Law and the prophets as love of God and neighbor, whose disciples taught that God is love—which casts out fear, is the fulfillment of the Law and does no harm to one's neighbor—is just not likely to manipulate with terror tactics those for whom he died.

Jesus reveals realities that are not immediately evident to us, and we know from our daily lives that reality frequently turns out to be stranger than it appears upon first glance. We believe and accept many things about this physical universe that initially seem implausible.

That the earth revolves around the sun or that the desk my elbows are resting on is composed of subatomic particles are truths not immediately apparent to me. But I accept these truths because they are part of the world picture of modern science. With the proper training and talent I, presumably, could personally discover these truths about the universe at some later time. For now I have faith in them based on the prestige and authority of modern science—not an unreasonable faith but not verified by my personal experience either. I've inherited an intellectual tradition and believe I have good, justifiable reasons to accept this tradition with its propositions about the cosmos.

So too with the facts of human destiny. Upon my death I will know directly about heaven and hell, but for now these truths are revealed to me by the Word of God. Jesus discloses what humanity's ultimate end will be, heaven or hell. And after all, some realities should be dreaded, just as others are to be marveled at.

The Wrath of God

The wrath of God is little mentioned today except in comedy clubs or Fundamentalist Anonymous groups. Here's a common thought: "People should respond to the love of God, not to his wrath."

True, but the person who can't be moved by either the love of others or fear of the law is called a sociopath. The inability to experience appropriate fear is psychologically and spiritually pathological. So by all means, preach the love of God, but leave room for his wrath, which is "never the capricious, self-indulgent, imitable, morally ignoble thing that human anger so often is. It is, instead, a right and necessary reaction to objective moral evil."[38]

Since we weren't created to perform moral evil, we were never intended to fall under the wrath of God.

> For God has not destined us for wrath, but to obtain salvation through our Lord Jesus Christ.... While we were yet helpless, at the right time Christ died for the ungodly.... God shows his love for us in that while we were yet sinners Christ died for us. Since, therefore, we are now justified by his blood, much more shall we be saved by him from the wrath of God. For if while we were enemies we were reconciled to God by the death of his Son, much more, now that we are reconciled, shall we be saved by his life. (1 Thessalonians 5:9; Romans 5:6, 8–10)

The Necessity of Retribution

Neglect of God's wrath follows pooh-poohing the concept of retribution or confusing vengeance and justice. Let's have none of the pretense that somehow we have evolved beyond the need for retributive justice. Let's avoid saying, "How much better to take a scoundrel and rehabilitate him," or, "If we must punish, then let's make sure it deters others."

Very well, but both rehabilitation and deterrence, if they aren't themselves to become immoral, depend on whether or not the person in our custody is guilty. To "rehabilitate" an innocent person against his will is unjust. To punish an innocent person as a lesson to others is wicked. But as soon as you ask, "Is he getting what he deserves?" you are acknowledging the necessary demand of retribution.

The legitimacy of "just desserts" depends on people's getting what they earned. We may disagree over what exactly constitutes the offense, but we all have the moral sense that evil men ought to reap what they sow, criminals ought to be punished for their crimes, and the head with its hangover is rightly judged for the previous night's excess.

Pope John Paul II wrote of this inherent moral sense:

> There is something in man's moral conscience itself that rebels against any loss of this conviction: Is not God who is Love also ultimate Justice? Can He tolerate these terrible crimes [concentration camps, gulags, suicide bombings, rapes, tortures and so forth], can they go unpunished? Isn't final punishment in some way necessary in order to reestablish moral equilibrium in the complex history of humanity?[39]

This cry for justice is a clue to our divine creation and our implicit awareness of the Supreme Judge of all that transpires on the face of the earth. Judgment at history's end climaxes the process by which God holds nations and persons accountable to him as Creator and Lord. The gospel is the Good News that through the Savior the requirements of divine justice have been met.

What Words Will We Hear?

By faith and baptism we are united with Christ. Our good works flow from this union. As they become habitual, good works increase our inclination to resist the evil attitudes and deeds that would drive us from the presence of God.

At the Second Coming God, in the person of Jesus Christ, will pronounce a definitive judgment upon the moral quality of each person's life. We hope to hear:

> "Come, O blessed of my Father, inherit the kingdom prepared for you from the foundation of the world; for I was hungry and you gave me food, I was thirsty and you gave me drink, I was a stranger and you welcomed me, I was naked and you clothed me, I was sick and you visited me, I was in prison and you came to me."... And the King will answer them, "Truly, I say to you, as you

did it to one of the least of these my brethren, you did it to me."
(Matthew 25:34–36, 40)

Here is what we rightly fear:

"Depart from me, you cursed, into the eternal fire prepared for the
devil and his angels; for I was hungry and you gave me no food,
I was thirsty and you gave me no drink, I was a stranger and you
did not welcome me, naked and you did not clothe me, sick and
in prison and you did not visit me." Then they also will answer,
"Lord, when did we see thee hungry or thirsty or a stranger or
naked or sick or in prison, and did not minister to thee?" Then he
will answer them, "Truly, I say to you, as you did it not to one of
the least of these, you did it not to me." (Matthew 25:41–45)

These are truly fearsome words, and "by the fear of the LORD
a man avoids evil" (Proverbs 16:6). Something is not quite right
when a man is afraid of nothing. Such fearlessness stems not
from courage but from a false interpretation of reality. It can
only be maintained by self-deception or a refusal to look at
natural or supernatural reality head-on.

It has become common to hear people say, "I'm a good
person," when challenged about their behavior. Apparently
they think that such self-characterization is a potent credential
to defuse or excuse any criticism we might offer of their
actions. But ultimately, even the "I am basically good" people
are not the best judges of themselves. Our motives are complex, and our desires run deep. We hardly know how our own
children regard us, never mind outsiders.

I simply don't see myself as I really am. I must have been
twelve or thirteen years old when I first heard my voice played
back on a tape recorder. (This was before handheld recorders,
videocams or the obsession with creating an audio and video
library of our kids from infancy until…uh, whenever.) I was
appalled. My voice sounded like a girl's, and the melody I

heard myself abusing was nothing like the one I heard in my head. It was shocking.

This is a simple analogy of what I may experience on Judgment Day, when I will see my entire life with an undeniable objectivity. Even Saint Paul, who was of rather robust conscience, wrote:

> But with me it is a very small thing that I should be judged by you or by any human court. I do not even judge myself. I am not aware of anything against myself, but I am not thereby acquitted. It is the Lord who judges me. Therefore do not pronounce judgment before the time, before the Lord comes, who will bring to light the things now hidden in darkness and will disclose the purposes of the heart. (1 Corinthians 4:3–5)

Are you pursuing your relationship with your Creator? Most of the same principles that govern human interpersonal relationships apply to our relationship with the Infinite-Personal God. We spend time with the people we love. Neglect a relationship, and we find ourselves growing distant from one another. The bumper sticker may sound flippant, but it makes a point: "If God seems distant, guess who moved."

Hell is the ultimate in distance from God. Communion with him is what we were made for. Jesus beckons us to know him: "Come to me, all who labor and are heavy laden, and I will give you rest.… For I am gentle and lowly in heart, and you will find rest for your souls" (Matthew 11:28, 29).

To know him is to love him. To love him is to further know him. His invitation stands, and the one who refuses it can claim to neither love nor know him. Such a person should fear hearing: "I never knew you" (Matthew 7:23).

Our expectation of judgment should not be wholly fear but holy fear. Catholic theologian Regis Martin writes: "It is not well to be without both a lively hope of getting to Heaven, which is the heart's deepest longing, and holy fear lest we get Hell instead, which will consist of a final sundering of man from God, the utmost catastrophe ever to threaten man, alongside of which even planetary disasters pale into insignificance."[40]

Part V

The Second Coming

What do Catholics believe about the Millennium?

Catholics don't think much about it. Over a three-year period Catholics going to Sunday Mass will hear over seven thousand verses of Scripture. The word *millennium* shows up in just one of those verses, because only one passage of the New Testament refers to a millennium by name. On the other hand, at every Sunday liturgy we confess in the Creed that Jesus "will come again to judge the living and the dead."

Developments within American Protestantism over the past 150 years have brought "the Millennium" into the cultural mainstream. The best-selling nonfiction book of the 1970s, secular or religious, was Hal Lindsey's *The Late, Great Planet Earth*. Since 1996 the fictional *Left Behind* series has sold over sixty million copies. Both books are built around events connected with the Millennium.

Millennium comes from the Latin *mille* ("thousand") and *annus* ("year"). It's theological shorthand for an era when all our aspirations for peace, justice, freedom and love will be realized through Christ's rule, as described in the Book of Revelation or Apocalypse (from the Greek verb *apokalypto*, "to reveal") chapter 20, verses 1–10:

> Then I saw an angel coming down from heaven, holding in his hand the key of the bottomless pit and a great chain. And he seized the dragon, that ancient serpent, who is the Devil and Satan, and bound him for a thousand years, and threw him into the pit, and shut it and sealed it over him, that he should deceive the nations no more, till the thousand years were ended. After that he must be loosed for a little while.
>
> Then I saw thrones, and seated on them were those to whom judgment was committed. Also I saw the souls of those who had

been beheaded for their testimony to Jesus and for the word of God, and who had not worshiped the beast or its image and had not received its mark on their foreheads or their hands. They came to life, and reigned with Christ a thousand years. The rest of the dead did not come to life until the thousand years were ended. This is the first resurrection. Blessed and holy is he who shares in the first resurrection! Over such the second death has no power, but they shall be priests of God and of Christ, and they shall reign with him a thousand years.

And when the thousand years are ended, Satan will be loosed from his prison and will come out to deceive the nations which are at the four corners of the earth, that is, Gog and Magog, to gather them for battle; their number is like the sand of the sea. And they marched up over the broad earth and surrounded the camp of the saints and the beloved city; but fire came down from heaven and consumed them, and the devil who had deceived them was thrown into the lake of fire and brimstone where the beast and the false prophet were, and they will be tormented day and night for ever and ever.

Interpreters of the Apocalypse generally espouse one of four basic beliefs about the events recorded there:

1. The events described are mostly in the past, usually the first century. This is held by many Catholics today, although most believe that the Second Coming is still future.

2. The events describe the grand sweep of history from the first century through the Last Judgment. This was very popular in the Protestant Reformation, when the papacy was interpreted as the whore of Babylon.

3. The events are primarily in the future. A number of early church fathers held this position, as did Saint Robert Bellarmine (1542–1621). It is popular among Catholics and

probably the dominant position in American Protestant evangelicalism.

4. The symbols, images and patterns describe nonhistorical, timeless truths to be realized in the soul.

Given that Scripture has several levels of meaning and that the church's teaching authority hasn't nailed down a particular one-to-one interpretation of all the symbolism, chronology or prophecy of the Book of Revelation, Catholics have considerable room to speculate, dispute and interpret this most difficult of books.

Christian thinkers have interpreted the Millennium in three different ways:

❖ premillennial: Christ returns before the Millennium.

❖ postmillennial: Christ returns after the Millennium.

❖ amillennial: Christ has already inaugurated the Millennium.

Premillennialism

Premillennialism teaches that Christ returns visibly and bodily *to earth* at some future time to bind Satan, raise a portion of the dead and set up an earthly kingdom, where he and the resurrected saints will rule in justice and peace for a literal thousand years. After the thousand years Satan will be released, and the millennial kingdom ends with a final rebellion and a reassertion of evil's hold on some human beings. Then Christ returns, defeats Satan, raises the remaining dead, conducts the Last Judgment and regenerates the heavens and earth.

This interpretation enjoys great popularity among Baptist, Brethren, Holiness, Pentecostal and so-called non-denominational Christians in America. Some important church fathers held a form of premillennialism for varying reasons.[1] The Catholic church, however, rejects the idea of Christ's physically reigning on the earth before his final return in glory.

Why does the Catholic church decline this notion? Because premillennialism puts all its evidential eggs in one biblical basket, Revelation 20! It doesn't sufficiently harmonize the teaching of the entire Bible, and it insufficiently considers the fact that the images in apocalyptic literature like the Book of Revelation are often symbolic rather than literal.

Premillennialists argue that a literal thousand years on the earth is necessary for God to fulfill his promises to Israel. David's throne must be reestablished if the Messiah is to rule from Jerusalem. The temple must be rebuilt, the priesthood and animal sacrifices renewed. The Catholic church teaches, however, that the New Testament doesn't interpret these promises in this literalistic manner. Rather all the Old Testament promises to Israel are fulfilled in Jesus and his church, the Israel of God, which is built on the foundation of the twelve apostles, corresponding to the twelve tribes of Israel (see 2 Corinthians 1:20; Galatians 3:29; 6:16; Ephesians 2:20; Revelation 21:14).

Further, Scripture gives us no warrant for splitting the Second Coming into two separate events distanced from each other by a thousand years. "When the Son of Man comes in his glory, and all the angels with him, then he will sit on his glorious throne. Before him will be gathered all the nations, and he will separate them one from another as a shepherd separates the sheep from the goats" (Matthew 25:31–32).[2] The return of Christ, the resurrection of the dead, the Last Judgment, the regeneration of the cosmos and the eternal state all take place concurrently, not consecutively.

Postmillennialism

Postmillennialism, the belief that Christ returns after the Millennium, is based on the conviction that Christ's death and resurrection bound Satan. As a result, evil imperceptibly but increasingly is losing its force. The "Millennium" refers to the present period of time, when the world is being transformed gradually by the successful preaching and practice of the gospel.

"Progress" is the key for postmillennialism. Christ's kingdom expands gradually but inescapably through history. Puritan divine Richard Baxter (1615–1691), in *The Glorious Kingdom of Christ, Described and Clearly Vindicated,* taught that the kingdom would not arrive cataclysmically at the return of Christ to earth but would grow in stages until it encompassed the whole world (see Matthew 13:31–33).[3]

Sometimes called "progressive millennialism," the idea found its greatest voice in America's most influential Protestant theologian, Jonathan Edwards (1703–1758), father of the First Great Awakening. By the mid 1800s Edwards's progressive millennialism dominated American Protestant leadership.

The Second Great Awakening in the first half of the nineteenth century emphasized not only personal conversion but social reform. Charles Finney (1792–1875), the most influential revivalist of his generation, urged Christians to perfect society. One's time and energy must be invested in establishing the millennial kingdom of God on earth by winning converts and involving oneself in the abolition of slavery, prohibition of alcohol, prison reform and other social initiatives.

In the generation after the Civil War, postmillennial optimism spawned the Social Gospel Movement, which remained vital from the 1880s through World War I. While later social gospel advocates still worked for a kingdom of heaven on earth, most thought in terms of the steady march of human progress and evolutionary process rather than the Christ-centered millennium of Edwards or Finney.

Millennarianism had grown secular; the Christian redemptive drama of history had been emptied of its meaning. "A God without wrath brought men without sin into a kingdom without judgment through the ministrations of a Christ without a Cross."[4]

Secular political experiments tried to create millennial utopias. The judgment of God was replaced by the wrath of state-sponsored coercion. The nineteenth-century liberal vision of the Fatherhood of God and the brotherhood of man deteriorated into the twentieth-century Marxist-Leninist paradise of the proletariat and the Nazi racist myth of the purified bloodline.

The Catholic church explicitly warns against identifying the fulfilled kingdom with any era of time, movement of men or reign of nations. The church has rejected "even modified forms of this falsification of the kingdom to come under the name of millenarianism, especially the 'intrinsically perverse' political form of a secular messianism" (*CCC*, #676).

Christ further teaches through his church that "the Kingdom will be fulfilled...not by a historic triumph of the Church through a progressive ascendancy, but only by God's victory over the final unleashing of evil...the Last Judgment after the final cosmic upheaval of this passing world" (*CCC*, #677; see Revelation 13:8; 20:7–12; 21:2–4; 2 Peter 3:12–13).

Too often those who believe that Christ's reign will be fully realized on earth see themselves as the agents to hasten his return and thus history's climax. It tempts us to identify our religious, national, social or cultural vision with the coming kingdom. But Christ's kingdom can only be established by his visible, bodily return (see Acts 1:11; 1 Thessalonians 4:16–17; Revelation 1:7). We cannot force the fulfillment before the Father's time.

Scripture teaches that evil is not progressively eliminated but must be continually struggled against up to the final push for victory at Christ's return. Even in the church, not to say the world, the wheat and the weeds grow alongside one another. Only at the end of history will the final separation of the just and the unjust be realized (see Matthew 13:24–30, 36–43; *CCC,* #681).

Postmillennialism envisions Christ's return to a world of flourishing faith and thriving Christian civilization. Yet this vision seems incompatible with the Lord's rhetorical question: "When the Son of man comes, will he find faith on earth?" (Luke 18:8). The expected answer is "No." The New Testament assumes a period of spiritual decline and persecution before the end, and special perseverance will be required from the few faithful. This is hardly a picture of a flourishing Christian culture. More Christians were martyred in the twentieth century than ever before.[5] This is progress?

Along these same lines, postmillennialism claims that the worst days of persecution, apostasy and the Antichrist are past (except for the brief Satan-led rebellion just before Christ's Second Coming). Not so.

> Before Christ's second coming the Church must pass through a trial that will shake the faith of many believers [see Luke 18:8; Matthew 24:12]. The persecution that accompanies her pilgrimage on earth [see Luke 21:12; John 15:19–20] will unveil the "mystery of iniquity" in the form of a religious deception offering men an apparent solution to their problems at the price of apostasy from the truth. The supreme religious deception is that of the Antichrist, a pseudo-messianism by which man glorifies himself in place of God and of his Messiah come in the flesh [see 2 Thessalonians 2:4–12; 1 Thessalonians 5:2–3; 2 John 7; 1 John 2:18, 22]. (*CCC,* #675)

Postmillennialism lost credibility after the rise of atheistic communism, National Socialism, the holocaust of the Jews, the two World Wars, the atomic bomb and so on. Our control of nature increased but not our self-control. Never has a century been so bloody as the twentieth. Progress wasn't inexcitable.

Amillennialism

The term *a-millennialism*—that is, "no millennium"—is misleading. What the amillennialists reject is a literalistic interpretation of the Millennium, not Revelation 20. They believe that the Millennium was inaugurated at the enthronement of Jesus Christ. So Christ's present "millennial" reign began with his ascension to the throne of God, fulfilling the promise that a son of David would always sit on the royal throne (see 2 Samuel 7:1–29; 23:5; Psalm 89:3, 28, 34, 39; 110; 132:11; Acts 2:30–32). Sometimes it is called "present millennialism" or "realized millennialism."

Satan was bound by Christ's death and resurrection in a decisive but not final victory over evil (see Colossians 2:15; Ephesians 1:16; 6:12; 2 Corinthians 4:14; Matthew 12:29; Luke 10:18; Romans 16:20). Christ bound Satan for a particular purpose: "that he should deceive the nations no more" (Revelation 20:3). After the Ascension, Christ was seated at the right hand of the Father, and the Holy Spirit was poured out on all the nations on Pentecost through a gift of speaking in tongues (beginning to reverse the curse from the Tower of Babel) and through the preaching of Saint Peter (Christ's beginning to build his church on the "rock" so that the gates of hell could not prevail) (see Acts 2; Matthew 16:17–19).

The universalist message that in Christ there is neither Jew nor Greek, neither bound nor free (see 1 Corinthians 12:13; Galatians 3:28), is central to this new move of God in first-century Judaism. Satan can no longer blind the eyes of the nations (gentiles) to the gift of Judaism to the world. This inexpressible gift is Christ the Messiah with all the cosmological, social and spiritual transformations that attend his coming. As Simeon said when Mary presented Christ in the temple, he would be "a light for revelation to the Gentiles" (Luke 2:32).

A new world was dawning, a new creation, a new universal and cosmic order of things, and Satan could not stop it. And as we now know, the Roman Empire was "converted," and the church became the first truly universal institution.

The church's universal preaching mission to the gentiles will go on for a symbolic thousand years—that is, an indefinite but "full" duration. Thus the Millennium is the whole interval of time from the resurrection of Christ to the final conflict—that is, the whole duration of the church, during which time the devil has lost the power to snuff out the Good News (see Matthew 12:29; Luke 10:18; Revelation 20:3).

Christ's reign and his kingdom have begun and are manifest in this world as people receive the Word of God in faith and are incorporated into the risen Christ by baptism. Even now God has "raised us up with Christ and seated us with him in the heavenly realm in Christ Jesus" (Ephesians 2:6). During his public ministry Jesus said that the time had already come when "the dead will hear the voice of the Son of God, and those who hear will live" (John 5:25; see also 16:33; Romans 6:1–8; 1 John 3:14; Revelation 20:4; 4:4). This is the "first resurrection."

When the gospel finally has been proclaimed to all the nations, Satan will be released and allowed to deceive the nations again "for a little while" (Revelation 20:3). Then Christ will return and defeat him absolutely. The dead will be raised, the Last Judgment will ensue, the redeemed will receive their glorified bodies, the unrepentant will enter the "second death," the eternal separation from God, and there will be the creation of the new heavens and earth (see 2 Peter 3:13; Revelation 21:1–2).

For amillennialists the kingdom of Christ is not intangible. It is factual, effectual, substantive and current. His kingdom is being extended and advanced through the preaching and practicing of the gospel by those who are happy slaves to his benevolent lordship. The kingdom of God is both a present reality and a future hope. It currently exists, so we pray that God's will be done on earth as it is in heaven, but it will not be fully realized until the creation of the new heaven and earth.

The Catholic Position

Variations and admixtures of these three basic positions have been proposed over the centuries. The Catholic church affirms that each of these interpretations contains some truth, but historically she has taught a version of amillenialism. Through the era commonly called "the church age" there will be a waxing and waning of success in preaching the gospel. There will be times of great persecution, wickedness and injustice and times when cultures may be more or less "Christianized"—that is, when the majority of men and women have come into union with Christ and have internalized the priorities of the kingdom, creating social institutions of justice and peace.

John Paul II urged Christians to work toward this civilization of love and to make Christ the heart of the world. You and I are the agents responsible for this moral and spiritual progress. This is not unaided human idealism but the work of the same Spirit of God who constituted the church from all nations, kindred and tongues on the Day of Pentecost.

Few passages of Scripture are as complicated and controversial as Revelation 20:1–10. No one questions, however, that it affirms that the devil's days are numbered and that Christ's final victory and Satan's final defeat will last "forever and ever." Amen.[6]

What does the church teach about "the rapture"?

The word *rapture* doesn't appear in the Bible. It is derived from the Latin *rapio*, meaning "caught up." Evangelical and fundamentalist Protestants who practice a theology called "Dispensationalism" have popularized the word. To them "the rapture" refers to a return of Christ to catch up the bodies of dead and living believers from the earth. Then follows a series of events lasting over a period of a thousand years before Christ returns in the Final Judgment. Catholics believe, on the other hand, that the "rapture" occurs at the end of human history; we use the word "general resurrection" to refer to that event.

Debates over end-time issues have been contentious. Even the esteemed *Evangelical Dictionary of Theology* concludes, "The interpretation of the rapture has introduced a divisive element into evangelicalism."[7]

Dispensationalists disagree over the timing of the rapture. Most believe that it occurs just before a seven-year period of tribulation. Others hold that the believers will be "caught up" midway through the Tribulation. Others believe that the rapture occurs at the end of the Tribulation period. There is even a partial rapture theory.

The doctrine was largely unheard of until the 1830s. The admittedly anti-Catholic, fractious Plymouth Brethren teacher

John Nelson Darby (1800–1882) offered a novel interpretation of Daniel 9:24–27. This metastasized into the sprawling system of biblical interpretation called Dispensationalism.

The exegetical details would take us too far afield of my purpose in this book. In short, Darby placed a "parenthesis" between Daniel's sixty-ninth and seventieth weeks. Israel's prophetic clock stopped—that is, the unfulfilled prophecies remained unfulfilled. The church was introduced as a "parenthesis" in history until the times of the gentiles were full. Then the seventieth week of Daniel begins with the rapture of the church. The prophetic clock begins ticking again.

The emerging interdenominational Bible prophecy conferences in the United States took notice, and from 1859 to 1874 Darby made seven trips to the United States and Canada. The trans-Atlantic evangelist Dwight Moody came under his sway.[8]

In the early twentieth century this scheme of interpretation was disseminated in the enormously popular *Scofield Reference Bible,* and Dallas Theological Seminary and Moody Bible Institute made its propagation part of their mission. When the United Nations created the modern state of Israel in 1948, interest intensified. The real estate to act out the "unfulfilled" prophecies was now under the control of the Jews.

But belief in a Darby-like "rapture" remained a minority position even among Christians of the last 150 years. It received spectacular attention through Hal Lindsey's *Late, Great Planet Earth,* the best-selling book of the 1970s. The fictitious *Left Behind* series, with sales of sixty million, is now circulating the same prophetic scenario. So dominant is this interpretive schema in some conservative Protestant circles that to disagree over some of its details constitutes reason to suspect the authenticity of a person's commitment to biblical authority.

While there are innumerable pieces to the dispensationalist jigsaw puzzle of prophecy, the New Testament text most commonly quoted in support of the rapture is 1 Thessalonians 4:13–17:

> But we would not have you ignorant, brethren, concerning those who are asleep, that you may not grieve as others do who have no hope. For since we believe that Jesus died and rose again, even so, through Jesus, God will bring with him those who have fallen asleep. For this we declare to you by the word of the Lord, that we who are alive, who are left until the coming of the Lord, shall not precede those who have fallen asleep. For the Lord himself will descend from heaven with a cry of command, with the archangel's call, and with the sound of the trumpet of God. And the dead in Christ will rise first; then we who are alive, who are left, shall be caught up together with them in the clouds to meet the Lord in the air; and so we shall always be with the Lord.

The dispensationalist interpretation of this passage maintains that there are two separate and chronologically distinct stages in the Second Coming of Jesus. The graves are opened, and the dead bodies of believers are reunited with their souls. Living believers on the earth are removed to meet the incoming Jesus in the air. Later, after the seven-year tribulation on the earth, the rise of Antichrist, a thousand-year period of peace and a final battle against Satan, follows the second stage of the Second Coming, when Christ comes "again to judge the living and the dead."

The dispensationalist interpretation is nowhere mentioned in the writings of the church fathers, the medieval theologians, the popes and saints through the ages or even the Protestant reformers. It is not reflected in the doctrinal statements of any of the major historic denominational traditions of Protestantism. Furthermore, it is almost exclusively an

American phenomenon, with some support in Great Britain. It lacks apostolicity, antiquity and universality.

Catholic, Eastern Orthodox and Protestant Christians have interpreted the 1 Thessalonians passage as referring to the general resurrection at the Second Coming, the climax of human history. The event sounds like a final one: "Thus, we shall always be with the Lord" has the tone of finality.

Because unbelievers are "left behind" after the rapture and before the final judgment, they have what amounts to a second chance to repent after the return of Christ. This doesn't square with Paul's statement in 1 Thessalonians 5:2, "For you yourselves know well that the day of the Lord will come like a thief in the night." Christ's coming will be an unanticipated judgment on those who have refused his grace but a welcome and expected redemption for those who have cooperated with him. "But you are not in darkness, brethren, for that day to surprise you like a thief" (5:4).

Some aspects of the rapture teaching affirm and others deny certain teachings of the Catholic church (see *CCC*, #668–677). Dispensationalists cannot be accused, however, of timidly avoiding preaching on Christ's Second Coming. Their teaching creates a sense of impending divine visitation that often leads to repentance.

In reaction to "rapture-mania," Catholic teachers often shy away from properly emphasizing the church's teaching on the last things. But a gospel message that mutes the divine truth that Christ is coming again to judge the living and the dead is an abbreviated gospel. It creates a vacuum into which erroneous speculations are sucked. Many modern Catholic teachers must realize this and return to preaching the full gospel.

W̶hat do Catholics believe about the Second Coming?

Let me start by turning my attention from the grand conclusion of human history to little ol' me. When I observe myself, I seem wired to move toward some end. With the exception of fatigue, I seem to be unceasingly pushing toward some future. My personal history seems to be aiming for something. Is this also true for the race as a whole? What is that end? Where is history going?

Sometimes I catch a glimpse of it. But I'm so embedded in my time, my generation, that I have to trust what God, who is outside of time, has revealed about it. That goal is eternal communion with the Triune God, a fellowship of divine Persons, and friendship with one another in a kingdom of creative work, enchanting beauty, brilliant knowledge, gleeful play, interpenetrating love and the purity of heart that God intends for his rational creatures.

I believe, along with all those who profess the Nicene Creed, that "he will come again in glory to judge the living and the dead, and his kingdom will have no end." The end of history is coming to meet me, even as I remain immersed in history. Jesus' promise to return and receive his people to himself is good news (see John 14:3). For history is going somewhere, human beings will reap what they sow, justice and mercy will prevail, and heaven is more than my imagination.

Without this doctrine of the Second Advent, our aspirations for communion and justice are too easily co-opted by naïve idealism, social causes and utopian movements that either counterfeit or merely imitate the Jesus kingdom. That kingdom, which is not of this world, will always resist being identified with or collapsed into those kingdoms that originate not in the will of God but in the will of fallen humanity. Christ's promise to come again with justice in his hand gives me an axe to strike the roots of any messianic pretenders like the Third Reich, the Age of Aquarius, evolutionary eugenics, the communist workers paradise, free-love millennialism, totalistic Islam or any one of the gaggle of movements and utopian humanisms that vie for my allegiance.

Good people fall for the tease of the counterfeit kingdom. Martin Heidegger, a great German existentialist philosopher, devoted his life to better serve the Fuehrer, whom he called the Savior. Arnold Toynbee called communism "Christianity gone awry," and many have written of the Reverend Hewlett Johnson, Dean of Canterbury, as just one of millions "whose pilgrimage road led to Moscow where he paid homage to the new Utopia being built by Lenin and Stalin...to become nothing short of the Kingdom of Heaven in the here and now."[9]

Only upon Jesus' return will the kingdom be fully actualized. But in the meantime...?

Christ's return is not just a future event; it is also a present reality. When Christ came to earth, he inaugurated his kingdom. When he ascended to heaven, he began his reign at the right hand of God, the Father who "put all things under his feet" (Ephesians 1:20–22). Through his body the church, he demonstrates his current reign by performing miraculous signs and wonders (see Mark 16:17–18), and he urges us to pray "thy kingdom come, thy will be done on earth as it is in heaven" (Matthew 6:10). This prayer spurs us to cooperate with Christ by destroying all that is hostile to divine justice and love. Our businesses, families, churches and leisure should make visible the priorities of the age to come.[10]

"Seek first his kingdom and his righteousness and all these things shall be yours as well" (Matthew 6:33). God's kingdom is so different, it's usually overlooked by those preoccupied with getting ahead, getting even or getting stoned—and, I suppose, even with those "getting saved" if their religion is toxic to loving others. Jesus compares his kingdom to insignificant leaven and mustard seed (see Matthew 13:31–33; Mark 4:30–32; Luke 13:18–21). Its size can be misleading; it may seem ordinary and unremarkable. But because of the character of its king, no kingdom is more significant than Christ's.

Not only do people enter the kingdom, the kingdom enters them! Christ's return also effects our full transformation. Our divine sonship will be fully manifest. By living in the light of the final goal of our redemption, we have a vantage point from which we can live in the world but not be conformed to it or any of its false promises. We are to "attain...mature manhood...of the stature of the fullness of Christ" (Ephesians 4:13). This is part of God's "plan for the fullness of time, to unite all things in him, things in heaven and things on earth" (Ephesians 1:10).

We are sustained by the coming of Christ eucharistically.

> The coming of Christ was "already" and "not yet": he had come already in the incarnation, and on the basis of the incarnation would come in the Eucharist; he had come already in the Eucharist, and would come at the last in the new cup that he would drink with him in the Father's kingdom. When the ancient liturgy prayed, "let grace come [or "let the Lord come"], and let the world pass away," its eschatological perspective took in both the final coming of Christ and his coming in the Eucharist. The eucharistic liturgy was not a compensation for the postponement of the parousia but a way of celebrating the presence of one who had promised to return.[11]

In the meantime, however, the presence of Christ in the church, in humankind and in the universe is a hidden, inchoate presence. Christ is already in the age to come; his body is fully transformed by the Holy Spirit. Our bodies, however, are still mortal and sinful. Thus a "gap," a disproportion between our state and his, persists. So even though he dwells in us and acts through us, we can perceive him only through faith.

It is helpful, then, to imagine his coming in glory not as a kind of space travel, the reversal of what happened at the Ascension, but rather as our transformation. "Beloved, we are God's children now; it does not yet appear what we shall be, but we know that when he appears we shall be like him, for we shall see him as he is. And every one who thus hopes in him purifies himself as he is pure" (1 John 3:2–3).

The change will take place in us, not in him. The disproportion between our state and his will disappear when the Spirit transforms this "lowly body" of ours into the likeness of his glorified body (Philippians 3:21). Then we will become his members in the full sense of the word, the extension of his glorified personal body. Then we see Christ as he is in his glory. By means of the Holy Spirit we dwell in him and he in us; and through Christ, with Christ and in Christ we will see the Father face-to-face and recognize him as our Father. We will then know reality.

Why is the promise of Christ's return an important article of Catholic doctrine?

Biblical spirituality might best be summarized by the simple phrase "living on a promise." Throughout salvation history God buoys his people along life's troubled waters on a raft of great and precious promises (see 2 Peter 1:4). By these we are oriented to our future and motivated to pursue life-changing union with his will.

Noah ordered his life according to the promise of the coming flood and built the ark to bring salvation to his household. Abraham and Sarah's lives received their meaning from God's promise that Abraham's offspring would be as numerous as the sands of the sea and the stars of the heaven. Moses was called to lead God's people into the Promised Land. God assured King David that a descendant would inherit his throne forever. Isaiah prophesied of a coming kingdom of love, peace and justice, and through the prophet Jeremiah God promised a new covenant.

As a tangible deposit, a surety that all these promises are being progressively fulfilled, the Holy Spirit of promise is given to those who believe in Jesus. In him God's promises receive a new affirmation, a fresh "yes" (see Acts 2:38; Romans 15:8; 2 Corinthians 5:5; Ephesians 1:14).

Consequently, the preaching of the apostles invites all people to a richer salvation than that granted Noah. The church becomes the universal family of God, embracing all nations, kindred and tongues, even beyond Abraham's wildest imagination. Heaven becomes the ultimate Promised Land of those united to Christ by faith and baptism. Christ's shed blood and broken body, now given in the Eucharist for the life of the world, institute Jeremiah's new covenant. The coming of Jesus inaugurates Isaiah's vision of the peaceable kingdom. Wherever he reigns in the hearts of his people, the kingdom exists and its priorities are in evidence.

Life moves toward the ultimate fulfillment of all these promises at the Second Coming. History began in an uncultivated garden but finds its glorious culmination in the heavenly city of the New Jerusalem. The human story has meaning and direction, and the Second Coming of Jesus writes the final chapter.

When will Christ return?

Christ's final coming could happen at any moment, and he specifically refused to date the time. Since his first coming Christians have been living in the final age of the world, "the last hour" (see Revelation 22:20; Mark 13:22–23; Matthew 24:36–44; 25:1–40; 1 Thessalonians 5:1; 1 John 2:18; 1 Peter 4:7).

At times, when people have grown weary of living in the expectation of Christ's return, they have claimed that his promised return was fulfilled in his resurrection from the dead or the sending of the Holy Spirit at Pentecost. Occasionally it is argued that his "return" refers to his coming to regenerate the individual at conversion. Some, like Jehovah's Witnesses, claim that he has already returned and set up headquarters in Brooklyn. But the teaching of the church and the Scripture and the overwhelming testimony of Christian history is that Christ's return will be personal, bodily, future, perceptible and unmistakable in fulfilling all the promises of God.

We know that his return is delayed until certain events occur. Second Thessalonians 2:3 tells us, "Let no one deceive you in any way; for that day will not come, unless the rebellion comes first, and the man of lawlessness is revealed, the son of perdition." We cannot establish a clear chronology or order of future events, though Christians since apostolic times have succumbed to the temptation to exact a timetable (see 2 Timothy 2:16–18).

Nor can we gauge in what measure and manner these "signs" will be fulfilled; they are suggestive, not definitive. For instance, over the last twenty-five years Christian publishing houses have released books identifying Jimmy Carter, Anwar Sadat, Ronald Reagan, George Bush, Mikhail Gorbachev, Saddam Hussein, Bill Clinton and a host of lesser names as Antichrists.

Abuse of prophecy, however, is no excuse for failing to study prophecy. Scripture, after all, does call our attention to a few preliminary signs:

❖ Before the return of Jesus we will see the universal proclamation of the gospel (see Matthew 24:14; Acts 1:8; Revelation 14:6).

❖ The original covenant people of God, the Jews, will recognize their Messiah after the full number of gentiles has been brought into the covenant (see Mark 23:29; Luke 21:24; Acts 3:19–21; Romans 11:12–26).

❖ A time of general disorder, distress and great tribulation will come upon the world. Even the church won't be spared. Persecution will increase, and those lacking spiritual discernment will fall away from the faith (see Matthew 24; Luke 18:8; 21:12; John 15:19–20; 1 Corinthians 7:26; 2 Thessalonians 2:1–3; 1 Timothy 4:1; 1 Peter 4:17; 1 John 2:18–23; 4:1–5).

❖ The Antichrist will arise and spread a religious deception, a false messianism in which "man glorifies himself in place of God and of his Messiah come in the flesh" (see 2 Thessalonians 2:3–12; 1 John 2:18, 22; 2 John 7; *CCC*, #675–77).

The Antichrist will claim to set up the kingdom on earth. According to Scripture, however, God's kingdom will not be fulfilled until the return of the King. The kingdom comes not by human progress but only by "God's victory over the final unleashing of evil, which will cause his Bride to come down from heaven. God's triumph over the revolt of evil will take the form of the Last Judgment after the final cosmic upheaval of this passing world" (*CCC*, #677).[12]

Even during the persecution that accompanies the church throughout its pilgrimage on earth, Christians are called to watch, wait and work in expectation of Christ's imminent coming (see Matthew 25; Mark 13:33–37; 2 Thessalonians 3:6–13). So the coming kingdom is already present in mystery on the earth (see Ephesians 4:11–13). "Christ dwells on earth in his Church" (*CCC*, #669). In each Eucharist we experience a coming of Christ and "are filled 'with every heavenly blessing and grace.'"[13] So we live between the kingdom already inaugurated and the kingdom not yet consummated.

Observant Catholics anticipate his return to bring justice to all mankind and liberate the creation from the burden sin has imposed on it. We long for the transformation of our weak bodies into his glorious body and his full conferring upon us of our divine lives, which are currently hidden with him in God (see Romans 8:19–22; Philippians 3:20–21). For these glorious reasons Catholics sing during the liturgy, "Christ has died. Christ is risen. Christ will come again," and continue to repeat the ancient Aramaic cry: *Maranatha*, "Come, Lord Jesus" (Revelation 22:20; see 1 Corinthians 16:22).

Notes

About this Book

1. G.K. Chesterton, *All Things Considered* (New York: Sheed & Ward, 1956), p. 141 as quoted in George J. Martin, et al., *The Quotable Chesterton* (New York: Doubleday, 1987) p. 325.

Introduction: Why do Catholics make so much of sin?

1. The deadly sins are often called "the capital sins" (Latin *caput*, meaning "head") because they are the source or fountainhead of other sins. These vices are normally listed as pride, envy, anger, sloth, avarice, gluttony and lust. They are not merely particular sinful acts but deep dispositions toward sin. They threaten moral goodness and our relationship with God and others in time and eternity.

2. Mortimer Adler, *Great Books of the Western World,* Robert Maynard Hutchins, ed. (Chicago: Encyclopedia Britannica, 1994) vol. 2, p. 561 as quoted in Paul E. Little, *Know Why You Believe* (Downers Grove, Ill.: InterVarsity Press, 1976), p. 22.

3. See Jason Boffetti, "How Richard Rorty Found Religion" in *First Things,* 143 (May 2004), pp. 24–30.

4. See Peter Singer, *Animal Liberation* (New York: Ecco, 2001). For the human responsibility to animals from a Christian perspective, see Matthew Scully, *Dominion: The Power of Man, the Suffering of Animals, and the Call to Mercy* (New York: St. Martin's, 2003).

5. George Bernard Shaw, "Back to Methuselah" (1921), part 1, act 1, "In the Beginning," in Dan H. Laurence, ed., *The Bodley Head Bernard Shaw: Collected Plays with Their Prefaces,* vol. 5, (London: Bodley Head, 1972), as quoted in *Columbia World of Quotations,* 1996.

6. Adapted from Pamela Rosewell Moore, *The Five Silent Years of Corrie ten Boom* (Grand Rapids, Mich.: Zondervan, 1986), p. 11.

7. Joseph Cardinal Ratzinger (Pope Benedict XVI) *Introduction to Christianity* (San Francisco: Ignatius, 1990), pp. 15–16.

Part I: Teaching Authority

1. Vatican II, Dogmatic Constitution on Divine Revelation, *Dei verbum,* November 18, 1965.

2. See James Tunsted Burtchaell, *Catholic Theories of Biblical Inspiration since 1810* (Cambridge: Cambridge University Press, 1969).

3. W.K. Hobart, *The Medical Language of St. Luke* (London: Longmans, Green, 1882; reprint Eugene, Ore.: Wipf and Stock, 2004); Adolf von Harnack, *Luke the Physician: The Author of the Third Gospel and the Acts of the Apostles,* J.R. Wilkinson, trans. (London: Williams & Norgate, 1911), pp. 13–17, 175–198; W.M. Ramsay, *Luke the Physician and Other Studies in the History of Religion* (London: Hodder & Stoughton, 1908; reprint Minneapolis, Minn.: James Family Publishing Co., n.d.), p. 58.

4. Galileo Galilei (1564–1642), "Letter to the Grand Duchess Christine (1615)," quoted in R.H. Popkin, ed., *The Philosophy of the 16th and 17th Centuries* (New York: The Free Press, 1966), p. 63.

5. Saint Jerome, "Commentary on Isaiah Prologue," quoted in *Dei verbum,* 25. See Leo XIII, Encyclical *Providentissimus Deus* (On the Study of Holy Scripture); Benedict XV, encylical *Spiritus Paraclitus* (On Saint Jerome); Pius XII, encyclical *Divino Afflante Spiritu* (On the Promotion of Biblical Studies).

6. D.A. Hagner, *Word Biblical Commentary: Matthew 14–28,* vol. 33B (Dallas: Word, 2002), p. 827.

7. Daniel J. Boorstin, *The Discoverers* (New York: Random House, 1983), 187.

8. James Donaldson and A.C. Coxe, eds., *Constitutions of the Holy Apostles* in *Ante-Nicene Fathers,* vol. VII, electronic version (Oak Harbor, Wash.: Logos, 1997), pp. 21–24.

9. Saint Thomas Aquinas, *Summa Theologia* I, 1, 10, ad 1. Quoted in *Catechism of the Catholic Church,* #116.

10. See Steven Kellmeyer, "How to Read Scripture Like Jesus and the Apostles" in *This Rock,* February 2000, pp. 13–15. For a book-length treatment see Mark Shea, *Making Senses Out of Scripture: Reading the Bible as the First Christians Did* (New York: Basilica, 1999).

11. C.H. Spurgeon, "Lecture One" in *Commenting and Commentaries: Two Lectures Addressed to the Students of The Pastors' College, Metropolitan Tabernacle* (London: Passmore and Alabaster, 1890).

12. See also 1 Corinthians 11:1; Philippians 4:9; 1 Thessalonians 1:6; 2:14; 3:7, 9; Hebrews 6:12; 13:17.

13. See Vatican I, *Dogmatic Constitution on the Catholic Faith,* 3; Pius XII, 1950 encyclical *Humani Generis* (Concerning Some False Opinions).

14. For a fuller discussion of this argument, see Al Kresta, *Why Do Catholics Genuflect? And Answers to Other Puzzling Questions About the Catholic Church* (Cincinnati: Servant, 2001), pp. 130–133.

15. The writings of the Fathers are easily accessible at www.newadvent.org/fathers/.

16. Louis Berkhof, *The History of Christian Doctrines* (Grand Rapids, Mich.: Baker, 1975), pp. 38–39.

17. Paul Johnson, *A History of Christianity* (New York: Athenaeum, 1980), p. 105.

18. As quoted in Johnson, p. 103.

19. Quoted in Peter Brown, *Augustine of Hippo: A Biography* (Los Angeles: University of California Press, 2000), p. 217.

20. F.L. Cross and E.A. Livingstone, eds. *The Oxford Dictionary of the Christian Church* (Oxford: Oxford University Press, 2nd edition, 1974), p. 286.

21. As quoted in Johnson, p. 132.

22. See two books by Mike Aquilina that offer the best popular introduction to the church fathers: *The Fathers of the Church: An Introduction to the First Christian Fathers* (Huntington, Ind.: Our Sunday Visitor, 1999) and *The Way of the Fathers: Praying With the Early Christians* (Huntington, Ind.: Our Sunday Visitor, 1999).

23. John Paul II, apostolic letter *Divini Amoris Scientia,* "Saint Thérèse of the Child Jesus and the Holy Face Is Proclaimed a Doctor of the Universal Church," 1, October 19, 1997.

24. To be declared a "doctor of the church," however, is not a declaration that the particular teacher is entirely immune from error.

25. *Divini Amoris Scientia,* 8.

26. Saint Augustine, *Confessions,* 1:1, Henry Chadwick, trans. (Oxford: Oxford University Press, 1991), p. 3.

27. Vatican II, Declaration on the Relation of the Church to Non-Christian Religions, *Nostra aetate,* October 28, 1965.

28. See also Wisdom 8:1; John 1:9; Acts 14:17; 17:26; Romans 1:18—2:16; 1 Timothy 2:4.

29. Quoting the *Roman Missal,* Good Friday intercessions.

30. Quoting Romans 11:26; Acts 3:19–21; Luke 21:24; Ephesians 4:13; 1 Corinthians 15:28.

31. See Daniel Ali and Robert Spencer, *Inside Islam: A Guide for Catholics* (West Chester, Pa.: Ascension, 2003).

32. Cardinal William Keeler, "How Mary Holds Christians and Muslims in Conversation," December 8, 1995, http://www.nccbuscc.org/seia/keeler.htm.

33. Michael Fitzgerald, Commission for Interreligious Dialogue, "Christ and the Other Religions," created in preparation for Jubilee Year 2000, available at www.vatican.va.

34. John Paul II, *Crossing the Threshold of Hope,* Vittorio Messor, ed. (New York: Alfred A. Knopf, 1994), p. 85.

35. John Paul II, *Crossing the Threshold of Hope,* p. 87.

36. Donald Mitchell and James Wiseman, *The Gethsemani Encounter: A Dialogue on the Spiritual Life by Buddhist and Christian Monastics* (New York: Continuum, 1999).

37. Congregation for the Doctrine of the Faith, Letter to the Bishops of the Catholic Church on Some Aspects of Christian Meditation, October 15, 1989, 12.

38. Congregation for the Doctrine of the Faith, *Declaration Dominus Iesus,* June 6, 2000, 22, quoting Pope John Paul II, encyclical *Redemptoris Missio,* 36.

39. Vatican II, Dogmatic Constitution on the Church, *Lumen gentium,* November 1964. See *CCC,* #846–848.

40. Some Scriptural examples are found in Genesis 12:1–3; 13:14–17; 26:24; Tobit 3:16–17; Isaiah 6; Matthew 1:20; 2:13; 17:1–8; 28:2–7; Mark 9:2–8; Luke 1:11–20, 26–38; 9:28–36; 24:4–7; Acts 9:3–9; 2 Corinthians 12:1–10; Revelation 1:8–20.

41. Quoted in Michael P. Green, *Illustrations for Biblical Preaching,* revised edition of *The Expositor's Illustration File* (Grand Rapids, Mich.: Baker, 1989).

42. Saint John of the Cross, *Ascent of Mount Carmel,* bk. 2, chap. 19, 10 in Allison Peers, trans., *The Complete Works of St. John of the Cross* (London: Burns, Oates and Washbourne, 1934), p. 155.

43. Teresa of Avila, *Interior Castle,* 6.9, as quoted in William Most, "Private Revelations and the Discernment of Spirits."

44. *Didache* 11:3–8, http://www.earlychristianwritings.com/text/ didache-roberts.html. The *Didache: The Teaching of the Twelve Apostles* is the oldest surviving church order. See 1 Corinthians 12:8–12; 2 John 10.

45. Quoted in Father Benedict Groeschel, *A Still, Small Voice: A Practical Guide on Reported Revelations* (San Francisco: Ignatius, 1993), p. 160.

46. *De canon.,* bk. III, chap. liii, no. 15; bk. II, chap. xxxii, no. 11. English translation: *Benedict XIV on Heroic Virtue,* vol. III, chap. xiv. Quoted in Groeschel, p. 28.

Part II: Salvation and Sacraments

1. Why confess to a priest at all is treated in Kresta, *Why Do Catholics Genuflect?* pp. 117–122.

2. Saint Padre Pio, *Immagini di Santità* (Mondadori, 1999), p. 74, as quoted in Cardinal Jose Saraiva Martins, Prefect of the Congregation for the Causes of Saints, "One With Christ, One With Sinners," accessible at www.ewtn.com/padrepio/priest/ Cross.htm.

3. Saint Jerome, *Commentary on Ecclesiastes,* 10, 11, in Migne, *Patrologia Latina,* 23, 1096; cited in *CCC,* #1456.

4. It is necessary to make some distinctions. In the sacrament of penance Christ through his priest objectively extends the forgiveness of God to a penitent. Spiritual direction is non-sacramental, doesn't require a priest and takes place in the context of prayer between two disciples of Christ, one of whom serves as guide, and with the aim of conversion. Spiritual direction presupposes a psychologically healthy person who wants help in spiritual growth.

   Therapy aims at healing some aspect of the personality in a doctor-patient relationship using professional techniques. One often enters therapy because of a crisis in one's life due to addictions, marital crisis, ego collapse, inability to experience interpersonal intimacy, impairment due to guilt, shame, grief, addiction and so on. Counseling aims at relief, improved performance and problem-solving rather than healing.

5. I have found it helpful to use Hector Munoz, *Will You Hear My Confession? How to Make a Good Examination of Conscience and a Good Confession* (Staten Island: Alba House, 1983). Also see John A. Kane, *How to Make a Good Confession: A Pocket Guide to Reconciliation with God* (Sophia Institute Press, 2001) and Frances Randolph, *Pardon and Peace: A Sinner's Guide to Confession* (San Francisco: Ignatius, 2001). For a sound but popular theology of confession, see Scott Hahn, *Lord, Have Mercy: The Healing Power of Confession* (New York: Doubleday, 2003).

6. See *CCC*, #1454; Exodus 20; Deuteronomy 5:6–21; Matthew 5—7; Romans 12—15; 1 Corinthians 12—13; Galatians 5; Ephesians 4—6.

7. Pope John Paul II, Homily on September 13, 1987, Westover Hills, San Antonio, Texas, as quoted in *Homiletic and Pastoral Review* (July 1988). See also Pope John Paul II's apostolic exhortation "Reconciliation and Peace," 1984.

8. Pliny the Younger, Letter to Trajan, 10:96; 7, around A.D. 112. Quoted in *Christian History: Worship in the Early Church*, electronic edition (Oak Harbor, Wash.: Logos, 1996). See also A.N. Sherwin-White, *The Letters of Pliny: A Historical and Social Commentary* (Oxford: Clarendon, 1966).

9. Justin Martyr, *First Apology*, chap. 67, in A. Roberts, J. Donaldson and A.C. Coxe, *The Ante-Nicene Fathers Vol. 1: Translations of the Writings of the Fathers down to A.D. 325*, electronic edition (Oak Harbor, Wash.: Logos, 1997).

10. See Jarøslav Pelikan, *The Christian Tradition: A History of the Development of Doctrine, Vol. 1: The Emergence of the Catholic Tradition (100–600)* (Chicago: University of Chicago Press, 1971), p. 146.

11. Augustine, "First Epistle to Januarius," 2:2 in Philip Schaff, ed., *The Confessions and Letters of St. Augustine with a Sketch of His Life and Work: Nicene and Post-Nicene Fathers*, vol. 1, electronic edition (Oak Harbor, Wash.: Logos Research Systems, 1997).

12. See a church order from the early 200s, the *Didascalia, 26.* Sources for the *Didaskalia* seem to be John 7:53—8:11; the *Didache*, the Letters of Ignatius, Justin Martyr's *Dialogue with Trypho*, and the Sibylline Oracles.

13. *The Union Haggadah: Home Service for the Passover* (New York: Central Conference of American Rabbis, 1923).

14. P. Evdokimov, *L'Orthodoxie* (Paris, 1959), 241, 208, as quoted in Timothy Ware, *The Orthodox Church* (New York: Penguin, 1982), p. 294.

15. See P. Maniyattu, *Heaven on Earth: The Theology of Liturgical Space-Time in the East Syrian Qurbana* (Rome: Mar Thoma Yogam, 1995), pp. 25–26; Scott Hahn, *The Lamb's Supper: The Mass as Heaven on Earth* (New York: Doubleday, 1999). Another Scripturally intensive look at the Eucharist is Stephen B. Clark, *Catholics and the Eucharist: A Scriptural Introduction* (Cincinnati: Servant, 2000). To understand how the early fathers understood the Mass, see Mike Aquilina, *The Mass of the Early Christians* (Huntington, Ind.: Our Sunday Visitor, 2001).

16. Augustine, *City of God,* 10:6, in Philip Schaff, ed., *Nicene and Post-Nicene Fathers of the Christian Church* (Grand Rapids, Mich.: Eerdmans, 1886). See John Chrysostom, "Homily on Hebrews," 17:13; *CCC, #1322.*

17. Irenaeus, *Against Heresies,* 3.3.3.

18. Clement of Rome, 1 Corinthians 44:4–5, 40–44. "[Clement] wrote in opposition to some young people of the Corinthian community who had deposed the officials there (bishops and presbyters, but not the deacons, who are simply mentioned)." (Siegmar Döpp and Wilhelm Geerlings, eds., *Dictionary of Early Christian Literature*, Matthew O'Connell, trans. [New York: Crossroad, 2000], p. 133). In some local churches Clement's letter was regarded as Scripture.

19. Ignatius of Antioch, *Letter to the Philadelphians,* 4.

20. *Didache* 14. The *Didache* uses the Greek term *thusia,* or "sacrifice," to describe the Eucharist.

21. Irenaeus, *Against Heresies,* 4.17.5.

22. Cyril of Jerusalem, *Catechetical Lectures,* 5:10.

23. John Chrysostom, *On the Priesthood,* 6:4.

24. J.N.D. Kelly, *Early Christian Doctrines* (New York: Harper and Row, 1960), p. 196.

25. Vatican II, Dogmatic Constitution on the Church, *Lumen gentium,* November 21, 1964, o. 11; see *CCC,* #1324–1327.

26. Kenneth L. Woodward, "Hail, Mary," in *Newsweek,* August 25, 1997, p. 50. In June of 1997 a Vatican theological commission gave a negative verdict to the question of defining Mary's maternal mediation. Dr. Mark Miravalle, who favors a definition, challenges the commission's conclusions. See his "Response to a Statement of the Pontifical Commission on Mary Coredemptrix" available at www.marymediatrix.com.

27. Quoted by Mark Miravalle, "A New Marian Dogma? Coredemptrix, Mediatrix of All Graces, Advocate" (Vox Populi Mariae Mediatrici, 1998), available at http://www.catholicculture.org.

28. Mark I. Miravalle, *Mary: Coredemptrix, Mediatrix, Advocate* (Santa Barbara: Queenship, 1995), pp. x, xi.

29. Miravalle, *Mary: Coredemptrix, Mediatrix, Advocate* 14, n. 67. See also Michael O'Carroll, *Theotokos: A Theological Encyclopedia of the Blessed Virgin Mary* (Wilmington: Michael Glazier, 1982), pp. 36, 296–297.

30. Pope Pius XII, "On the Mystical Body" *Mystici Corporis Christi,* 1943, 110, www.adoremus.org/MysticiCorporisChristi.html.

31. John Paul II, *Salvifici Doloris,* "On the Christian Meanings of Human Suffering," February 11, 1984, 25, available at www.vatican.va.

32. John Paul II, address at Alborada, Guayguil, Ecuador, January 31, 1985.

33. See John Macquarrie, *Mary, Mother for All Christians* (Grand Rapids, Mich.: Eerdmans, 1991), pp. 112–113.

Part III: Worship and Devotion

1. See Exodus 20:6; Deuteronomy 5:15; Psalm 111; Isaiah 46:8–9; Luke 22:19; 1 Corinthians 11:24–26; 2 Peter 1:12.

2. Vatican II, *Sacrosanctum Concilium,* The Constitution on the Sacred Liturgy, December 4, 1963, chap. 5, no. 102.

3. Geoffrey Wainwright, "Beginning with Easter" in *The Reformed Journal* 38:3 (March 1988), p. 13.

4. These Jewish feasts are recorded in Scripture: Passover (Exodus 23:14; Leviticus 23:4–14); Rosh Hashanah (Numbers 29:1; Leviticus 23:23–25); Pentecost (Exodus 23:16; Leviticus 23:15–21; Numbers 28:26–31); Yom Kippur (Leviticus 23:26–32); Hanukkah (1 Maccabees 4:36, 59).

5. See "The Lord's Day" and "The Eighth Day" in Jean Danielou, *The Bible and the Liturgy* (Notre Dame, Ind.: Notre Dame University Press, 1956), pp. 242–286; Joseph A. Komonchak, Mary Collins and Dermot A. Lane, eds., "Names for the Christian Sunday," *The New Dictionary of Theology,* electronic edition (Collegeville, Minn.: Liturgical, 2000).

6. *Didache* 8:1; Apostolic Constitutions, 5.15.

7. Congregation for Divine Worship and the Discipline of the Sacraments, May 23, 2000, www.ewtn.com/Devotionals/mercy/feast.htm.

8. Thomas Howard, *Evangelical Is Not Enough* (Nashville: Thomas Nelson, 1984), p. 133.

9. "The Practice of the Christian Churches" in R. Webber, *The Services of the Christian Year,* electronic edition (Nashville: Star Song, 1994).

10. Jerry L. Sandige, "Assemblies of God Churches" in Webber.

11. General Norms for the Liturgical Year and the Calendar, 8–15.

12. The word *Easter* probably has roots in the Norse term *Eostur,* the season of the rising sun or the time of the new birth of spring.

13. The Philocalian Calendar (c. 354) lists the death and burial dates of the Roman martyrs and bishops. This may be our earliest example of a Proper of the Saints.

14. In the New Testament *parousia* can apply to men (see 1 Corinthians 16:17; 2 Corinthians 7:6; 10:10; Philippians 1:26; 2:12); the Antichrist (2 Thessalonians 2:9); or most commonly, Christ (see Matthew 24:3, 27, 37, 39; 1 Corinthians 15:23; 1 Thessalonians 2:19; 3:13; 4:15; 5:23; 2 Thessalonians 2:1, 8).

15. See Esther 4:1; Isaiah 58:5; Jeremiah 6:26; 25:34; Ezekiel 27:30; Daniel 9:3; Jonah 3:6; 1 Maccabees 3:47; Matthew 11:21; Luke 10:13.

16. See Komonchak, Collins and Lane; Justin Martyr, *Dialogue with Trypho,* chap. 41; Danielou, 257.

17. "In the Western Church, liturgy includes all the sacraments (including Eucharist), the Liturgy of the Hours (sometimes called the Divine Office), funerals, the rites for religious profession, ordination, the blessing of persons (abbots, abbesses), as well as the consecration of persons (virgins) and things (churches)." (M. Downey, *The New Dictionary of Catholic Spirituality* [Collegeville, Minn.: Liturgical, 2000], pp. 602, 603.)

18. Pliny, *Epistle to Trajan,* 10, 96, cited by G.J. Cuming, "The First Three Centuries," in Cheslyn Jones, et al., *The Study of the Liturgy* (New York: Oxford University Press, 1978), p. 353.

19. Cuming, in Jones, p. 353.

20. W. Jardine Grisbrooke, "The Formative Period: Cathedral and Monastic Offices" in Jones, p. 358.

21. Jones, p. 352. Also see Alexander Schmemann, *Introduction to Liturgical Theology* (London: Faith, 1966), p. 107.

22. General Instruction of the Liturgy of the Hours,

pp. 104, 106.

23. For a fine summary of "The Office in the West: Roman Rite" and its revision see J.D. Crichton in Jones, pp. 383–389.

24. Catholic Book Company publishes a four-volume edition containing complete texts for all the hours, feasts and seasons of the liturgical year. The Daughters of Saint Paul and Catholic Book Company both publish a one-volume edition called *Christian Prayer.*

25. Pope Paul VI, *Laudis canticum,* "Apostolic Constitution Promulgating the Revised Book of the Liturgy of the Hours," November 1, 1970. See canon 1173.

Part IV: Hell

1. Jeffrey L. Sheler, *U.S. News and World Report,* January 31, 2000, pp. 45–50.

2. See Council of Orange II (A.D. 529); Council of Trent (1547): 1567. For a fuller discussion of mortal sin see Kresta, *Why Do Catholics Genuflect?* pp. 94–97; *CCC,* #1854–1864.

3. Michael Glazier and Monika K. Hellwig, eds., *The Modern Catholic Encyclopedia* (Collegeville, Minn.: Litugical 1994), p. 375.

4. Pope John Paul II, *Crossing the Threshold of Hope,* p. 186.

5. See T.S. Eliot, *Four Quartets* (New York: Harcourt, Brace and World, 1943), p. 14.

6. Joseph Cardinal Ratzinger (Pope Benedict XVI), *Eschatology: Death and Eternal Life,* Michael Waldstein, trans. (Washington, D.C.: Catholic University Press, 1988), p. 215.

7. Wesleyan philosopher Jerry Walls's *Hell: The Logic of Damnation* (South Bend, Ind.: University of Notre Dame Press, 1992) was the source for much of this section.

8. Walls, p. 121.

9. Hannah Arendt, *Eichmann in Jerusalem: A Report on the Banality of Evil* (New York: Viking, 1964).

10. Søren Kierkegaard, *The Sickness Unto Death,* Walter Lowrie, trans. (Princeton, N.J.: Princeton University Press, 1941), p. 220.

11. M. Scott Peck, *People of the Lie* (New York: Simon and Schuster, 1983), pp. 47, 71.

12. Richard Swinburne, "A Theodicy of Heaven and Hell," in *The Existence and Nature of God,* Alfred J. Freddoso, ed. (Notre Dame, Ind.: University of Notre Dame Press, 1983), pp. 48–49.

13. Eric Harris, journal entry, 1999, http://columbine.free2host.net/eric/writing.html. While his motives, the role of parents, "goth" culture, bullies and so forth remain unclear, this excerpt from Harris's diary makes the point: People can develop a taste for and enjoy, even savor, wickedness.

14. C.S. Lewis, *Screwtape Letters* (San Francisco: Harper, 1996), p. 61.

15. Thomas Howard, *The Novels of Charles Williams* (San Francisco: Ignatius, 1991), p. 18.

16. *Life and Doctrine of Saint Catherine of Genoa* (New York: Christian Press Association, 1907), chap. 27.

17. C.S. Lewis, *The Problem of Pain* (New York: Macmillan, 1962), pp. 118–119.

18. Peter Kreeft and Ronald K. Tacelli, *Handbook of Christian Apologetics* (Downers Grove, Ill.: InterVarsity Press, 1994), p. 294. For a dynamic portrayal of how our choices form us for eternity, see C.S. Lewis, *The Great Divorce.*

19. Michael Sheehan, *Apologetics and Catholic Doctrine* (London: Saint Austin, 1918, 2001), p. 629.

20. Fulton Sheen, *The Quotable Fulton Sheen: A Topical Compilation of the Wit, Wisdom, and Satire of Archbishop Fulton J. Sheen* (New York: Doubleday, 1989), p. 125.

21. John Milton, *Paradise Lost* (New York: Penguin, 2003), p. 263.

22. John Wesley, *Works* (1872), 10:235; see *Works* (1985), 2:540–541 as quoted in Walls, p. 87.

23. John Paul II, general audience address, July 28, 1999, *L'Osservatore Romano*, August 4, 1999, Vatican.

24. Thomas Aquinas, Summa Theologiae, Ia2ae.87, 4, as quoted in Robert A. Peterson, "A Traditionalist Response to John Stott's Arguments for Annihilationism," in *Journal of the Evangelical Theological Society*, vol. 37, (1994; 2002), p. 563.

25. See John 3:29; Romans 7:4; 2 Corinthians 11:2; Ephesians 5:25–27, 29, 32; 1 John 4:8; Revelation 19:6–9; 21:2. In contrast, infidelity to God is corresponded with infidelity in marriage. See Exodus 34:12–16; Leviticus 20:5–6; Isaiah 1:21; Jeremiah 3:1–10; Ezekiel 6:9; 16:30–32; Hosea 9:1; 2 Corinthians 11:3; Revelation 17:1–5.

26. Lewis, *The Problem of Pain*, pp. 127–128.

27. For a fuller discussion of purgatory, see Kresta, *Why Do Catholics Genuflect?* pp. 98–102.

28. Peterson, p. 563.

29. Quoted in Walls, p. 111.

30. Lewis, *The Problem of Pain*, p. 128.

31. George MacDonald, "Kingship," *Christian Classics Ethereal Library at Calvin College*, /www.ccel.org/m/macdonald/unspoken3/htm/vii.htm.

32. Fulton J. Sheen, *The Life of All Living* (Garden City, N.Y.: Doubleday, 1979), p. 199.

33. See John Hardon, s.j., *Catholic Catechism: A Contemporary Catechism of the Teachings f the Catholic Church* (New York: Doubleday, 1981), p. 272.

34. Frank Herbert Brabant, *Time and Eternity in Christian Thought* (London: Longmans Green, 1937), p. 42. Quoted in C.F.H. Henry, *God, Revelation, and Authority* (Wheaton, Ill.: Crossway, 1999), vol. 5, p. 243.

35. See Romans 16:26; 1 Timothy 6:16; 1 Peter 5:10; Hebrews 9:14; 9:12; 5:9. Compare 2 Peter 1:11 with Luke 1:33; John 3:16 with John 10:28; 2 Corinthians 5:1 with 1 Corinthians 15:53, Matthew 25:46 with Titus 1:2. See also Mark 3:29; Hebrews 6:2; Matthew 18:8; 25:41; Jude 7; Mark 9:43.

36. C.S. Lewis, *Mere Christianity* (San Francisco: Harper, 1952), p. 74.

37. Kreeft and Tacelli, p. 300.

38. J.I. Packer, *Knowing God* (Downers Grove, Ill.: InterVarsity Press, 1973), p. 136. See John 3:36; Romans 1:18; 9:22; Ephesians 5:6; Colossians 3:6; 2 Thessalonians 1:7–9; Revelation 6:16; 11:18; 14:10; 16:19; 19:15.

39. John Paul II, *Crossing the Threshold of Hope*, p. 186.

40. Regis Martin, *The Last Things: Death, Judgment, Heaven, Hell* (San Francisco: Ignatius, 1998), p. 116.

Part V: The Second Coming

1. See Charles E. Hill, *Regnum Caeolorum: Patterns of Millennial Thought in Early Christianity* (Grand Rapids, Mich.: Eerdmans, second edition, 2001).

2. See Mark 14:62; Luke 9:26; John 5:28–29; 6:40; Acts 2:20–21; 1 Corinthians 1:8; 3:13; 5:5; Philippians 3:20–21; 2 Thessalonians 1:7–9; 2 Timothy 1:18; 4:8; Hebrews 9:27–28; 1 Peter 5:4; 2 Peter 3:10–13.

3. Richard Baxter, *The Glorious Kingdom of Christ, Described and Clearly Vindicated* (London: Parkhurst, 1691).

4. H. Richard Niebuhr, *The Kingdom of God in America* (New York: Harper & Row, 1959), p. 193.

5. See Robert Royal, *The Catholic Martyrs of the Twentieth Century: A Comprehensive World History* (New York: Crossroad, 2000). Protestant and Orthodox martyrs there are aplenty. Given the many different institutional affiliations, however, their number is more difficult to calculate. No single book, to my

knowledge, provides an overview of Protestant and Orthodox martyrs of the twentieth century, as does Royal for Catholics.

6. See Eduardo Arens Kuckerlkorn, Manuel Diaz Mateos and Tomas Kraft, "Revelation" in William R. Farmer, ed., *The International Bible Commentary: A Catholic Commentary for the Twenty-First Century* (Collegeville, Minn.: Liturgical, 1998), p. 1870.

7. R.G. Clouse, "Rapture of the Church" in Walter A. Elwell, *Evangelical Dictionary of Theology* (Grand Rapids, Mich.: Baker, 1984), p. 910.

8. Paul Thigpen, *The Rapture Trap* (West Chester, Pa.: Ascension Press, 2002), pp. 129–48 offers a sweeping survey of Christian history tracing the emergence of the rapture doctrine. Of special interest to Catholics is Thigpen's observation that a Chilean Jesuit, Manuel Lacunza, was a link in the chain of error. He influenced Edward Irving, a minister of the Protestant Church of Scotland, who was later excommunicated from his denomination for teaching that Christ's human nature was sinful. Historians debate whether Irving or Darby deserves more credit for introducing the doctrinal novelty to English-speaking Christendom.

9. See Paul Johnson, *Modern Times: The World from the Twenties to the Eighties* (New York: Harper and Row, 1983), pp. 276, 545.

10. See Romans 13:11–14; 1 Corinthians 7:26; 10:11; 15:51; Ephesians 4:30; Philippians 1:6, 9; 2:12–16; 4:15; 1 Thessalonians 2:19; 4:15; 2 Corinthians 7:1; 1 Timothy 6:14; 2 Timothy 1:12, 18; 4:18; Titus 2:13; Hebrews 10:23–25, 37.

11. Pelikan, pp. 126–127.

12. See Revelation 13:8; 19:1–9; 20:7–10, 12; 21:2–4; 2 Peter 3:12, 13. See also Vincent P. Micelli, *The Antichrist* (Fort Collins, Col.: Roman Catholic Books, 1981).

13. *CCC,* #1402–1404, quoting *Roman Missal,* Eucharistic Prayer I (Roman Canon), p. 96.

*I*ndex